D0949635

THE PROXIMITY PRINCIPLE

For you created my inmost being;
you knit me together in my mother's womb.

PSALM 139:13

THE PROXIMITY PRINCIPLE

*The Proven Strategy that Will
Lead to the Career You Love*

KEN COLEMAN

RAMSEY
PRESS

Published by Ramsey Press, The Lampo Group, LLC
Brentwood, Tennessee 37027

This publication is designed to provide accurate and authoritative information
with regard to the subject matter covered. It is sold with the understanding
that the publisher is not engaged in rendering financial, accounting, or other
professional advice. If financial advice or other expert assistance is required,
the services of a competent professional should be sought.

Scripture quotations are from the Holy Bible, New International Version®,
NIV®, Copyright © 1973, 1978, 1984, 2011 by Biblica, Inc.® Used by
permission of Zondervan. All rights reserved worldwide.

Book Development: Matt Litton, Preston Cannon, and Cathy Shanks
Editing: Amanda Johnson, Ami McConnell Abston, and Jen Gingerich
Cover Design: Brad Dennison and Chris Carrico
Interior Design: Mandi Cofer

ISBN: 978-0-978562-03-8

Printed in the United States of America
19 20 21 22 23 WRZ 5 4 3 2 1

DEDICATION

To Stacy, proximity to you has made me a
better man and this life an incredible journey.

To our children Ty, Chase, and Josie, you
make us so proud. May you practice this on
your journey to fulfill your purpose.

To my parents, thank you for your love and
the sacrifices you made to get me in proximity
to people and places that molded me.

CONTENTS

PART 2: THE PLACES 85

PART 3: THE PRACTICES 153

FOREWORD
Dave Ramsey

When I was about twelve, I asked my dad for some money to go with my buddies down to the local convenience store. I'll never forget his response.

"You don't need money. You need a *job!*"

Next thing I knew, I was knocking on doors all over Antioch, Tennessee. Whenever someone would answer, I'd hand them one of my business cards and request the "privilege" of serving their lawn care needs.

Pretty soon *Dave's Lawns* had dozens of clients, and I spent a blazin' hot summer cutting what seemed like every blade of grass in my entire neighborhood.

Of course, I've had a few jobs since then. I started selling real estate right out of high school and through college. And if you know my story, you know that I made a lot of money as young man, lost it all, then with God's help, built Ramsey Solutions from the ashes of my bankruptcy.

It's been a wild ride! And a lot of work. But hard work is something the Ramseys have been known for through the years. In fact, our family crest includes two Latin words. The first is *pray*. And the other is *work*.

Plus, as a Christian, I believe that work is a blessing, not a curse. In the earliest chapters of the Bible, Adam and Eve have a job to do—taking care of a garden. God gave those first people a purpose through work *before* sin entered the world. And He still wants people to find purpose in their work today.

That's right! God wants you to find something you love and do it for His glory—not just settle for a J-O-B and a paycheck.

If you're reading this book, I'm guessing you aren't afraid of hard work either. You're willing to put in the hours to really win at what you do—as long as what you do has purpose. You're looking for work that matters.

And that's where Ken Coleman comes in.

Ken is a man of many talents. For example, he's a world-class interviewer, having gone one-on-one with some of the biggest names you can imagine. He's talked with business leaders and successful coaches, prominent pastors, and former presidents. And absolutely *nobody* does it better!

That's one reason we asked him to join our team!

But I'll let you in on a secret: Ken's greatest passion is helping others discover their own passions—especially when it comes to their careers. Sure, he makes interviewing dignitaries and speaking to crowds and hosting his own radio show look easy. But Ken has worked his way through the ranks, and he knows from personal experience what it takes to turn a dream into reality.

In other words, he's been where you are—and he can help you get where you're wanting to go.

That's really what *The Proximity Principle* is all about.

Have you ever noticed you become who you hang around with? If you hang with readers, you'll read. If you surround yourself with people training physically, you will too. We even talk like the people we hang around. Our accents, dialects, and sentence structure reflect who we spend the most time with. For this reason, we don't let our children run with kids who misbehave because we quickly see that bad behavior in our children. It should come as no shock to you, then, that to get into and excel in a field, you need to be in the proximity of people who are in that same field.

I have used this principle unknowingly to shape my speaking style, learn to write, do a radio show, be a successful husband and parent, and lead our company. The people around me have made deposits into my life over the decades that have paid huge dividends, and I am grateful. Be in proximity to what you want to be. Wow. It sounds so simple, but there *is* more. You *can* live the life you want.

And Ken uses the "Proximity Principle" to show you how to make that happen.

One of my favorite quotes comes from automotive icon Henry Ford: "Whether you think you can or think you can't, you're right." I've shared that with audiences across America because it's absolutely true. Change is always possible in your life and in your career, but that change *always* depends on you.

And I can't think of anyone more qualified to guide you toward that change than Ken Coleman. So dive in and put *The Proximity Principle* to work. I believe it has the power to transform your career.

And your life.

ACKNOWLEDGMENTS

I am living my dream. Countless people have played roles in this book becoming a reality, but none more than Dave Ramsey. Dave, your belief, support, and generosity mean more to me than I can describe. Thank you for the opportunity to work on the Ramsey Solutions team. It is an honor to serve with you on this crusade.

Preston Cannon, your support for this content and leadership of the process has been invaluable. Thank you for the many brief huddles along the way.

Matt Litton, it was a privilege to lock arms with you on this book. Thank you for your work, the constant encouragement, and for your passion for the message.

Jen Gingerich, Cathy Shanks, Rick Prall, and Michelle Grooms—this book could not have happened without your skills, guidance, and commitment to excellence.

Chris Carrico, it was so much fun working with you as you led the collaboration on the book cover.

Elizabeth Cole and McKenzie Masters, thank you for your tireless and effective work to help me help others.

Suzanne Simms and Cody Bennett, thank you for your leadership and support as this idea became a book.

Bill Hampton, Jeremy Breland, and Les Parrott, you model the way, challenge me, and cheer me on.

Ty, Chase, and Josie, your questions, excitement, and prayers inspired me.

Stacy, your love, belief, prayers, and constant affirmation are a big reason why this book and everything I do happens. I cannot imagine being on this journey without you.

INTRODUCTION

If it is to be, it is up to me.

—WILLIAM H. JOHNSEN

Every one of us wants to do work that matters—work that aligns with our personal values, talents, and passions. Work that makes a difference in the world. Yet 70 percent of employees report they are completely dissatisfied with their current work situation.[1] Seventy percent! That means millions of people face each day with zero desire or excitement about their jobs.

The question is: *Why?*

Why do millions of people go through the work week like zombies waiting for the weekend? Don't misunderstand. Those 70 percent aren't indifferent. Many

1

are excellent employees. They just feel stuck in a job they are not passionate about. So why do so many people avoid taking that first step to a job they love? The problem is fear, pride, or plain old confusion about how to get started on their journey to a dream job.

I can tell you story after story of people who used to be part of that miserable 70 percent. Like my friend Jim, who spent forty years running his family furniture store instead of pursuing his passion for law. Or Rachel, who spent ten years in a banking career, daydreaming of being an event planner. And Noah, a sales executive in his thirties who always wanted to coach high school football. All three of them had a longing to chase their dreams and do more.

> EVERY ONE OF US WANTS TO DO WORK THAT MATTERS.

I understand that feeling because I have been there.

SOMETHING HAD TO CHANGE

For years I'd dreamed of being a broadcaster, but I was also one of the 70 percent—stuck in a job I didn't love.

Then one morning it hit me.

I was sitting on my back patio, coffee in hand, staring into the woods behind my house. I was lost and completely frustrated. All I could think about was the distance between where I was and where I wanted to be. My mind was racing. *Is it too late to start? And if it isn't too late, what if I try and fail? What will my wife, family, and friends say if I quit my job to try something new? Is a broadcasting career even possible for me?* To be perfectly honest, I was ashamed that I hadn't made any progress toward my goal. I knew something had to change.

My Dream and My Dream Alone

Then it came to me. My dream was real to me and only me. I was fully expecting someone to just drop a broadcasting job in my lap. When that didn't happen, instead of doing something about it, I decided to throw myself a pity party. The truth is, no one in the entire world was sitting on their back patio thinking about how they could help Ken Coleman get his dream job.

It was my dream and my dream alone.

That realization was both frightening and freeing. It was frightening because I knew if I was ever going to be a broadcaster, I was the only one who could make it happen. And it was freeing because it gave me just the kick in the butt I needed to stop feeling sorry for myself and start doing whatever it took to chase my dream.

Man, I was fired up! But I was also a little scared. Okay, *a lot* scared. Over the next few days as I was processing what had happened, I remembered a passage I read once by William Hutchison Murray that gave me the courage I needed to press on:

Until one is committed, there is hesitancy, the chance to draw back, always ineffectiveness. Concerning all acts of initiative (and creation), there is one elementary truth, the ignorance of which kills countless ideas and splendid plans: that the moment one definitely commits oneself, then Providence moves too. All sorts of things occur to help one that would never otherwise have occurred. A whole stream of events issues from the decision, raising in one's favor all manner of unforeseen incidents and meetings and material assistance, which no man could have dreamt would have come his way. I have learned a deep respect for one of Goethe's couplets: Whatever you can do, or dream you can, begin it. Boldness has genius, power, and magic in it![2]

Murray was a Scottish mountain climber in the 1930s. He became famous for winter climbing in the Western Highlands.[3] Can you imagine the determination and skill it takes to climb mountains? In the *winter*? As I thought about Murray's words, I realized that chasing after your dream job is a lot like climbing a mountain. Both require bravery. Both require that you have the right people around to help you. Both require that you learn as you go. And ultimately both require that you take one bold step at a time.

One Bold Step at a Time

That first step toward a dream job is *always* the scariest. My friend Jim took that first step by enrolling in law classes at the age of fifty-two. Rachel used her evenings to work as an intern at a local event company. And Noah went back to school and began volunteering after work with a local high school football team.

Me? I got off the patio and began pursuing my own dream job. It wasn't always easy. There were days—weeks even—when I felt scared, crazy, and hopeless. Other days I'd go from feeling excited and full of momentum to wondering if I should just give up. But I pressed on, and each step I took up the mountain got me in closer proximity to where I wanted to be. And now, seven years later, I've reached the summit! I'm the host of my very own daily radio show, *The Ken Coleman Show,* where I get to help other people get closer to their dream job.

> THAT FIRST STEP TOWARD A DREAM JOB IS *ALWAYS* THE SCARIEST.

Are you one of the 70 percent? Do you dread going to work each day because you're not passionate about your job? Are you looking up at your personal "Mount Everest," unsure of how to take the first step? The plan outlined in this book can help you reach the summit. And here's the exciting truth: finding opportunities to do what you love is as simple as getting around the right *people* and being in the right *places*. This is what I call The Proximity Principle.

So if you're ready to take that first bold step, let's begin it now.

CHAPTER 1

WHAT IS THE PROXIMITY PRINCIPLE?

The first step toward success is taken when you refuse to be a captive of the environment in which you first find yourself.

—MARK CAINE

Let's take a minute to talk about the word proximity. *Proximity* simply means to be near or close to something. When you are closer to something, it is often easier to access that thing, isn't it? That's not a hard concept. It isn't rocket science. It's actually common sense. It's just that common sense isn't so common.

And when you're far away from where you want to be, it makes things more difficult and challenging, right? I

experienced this that morning on my patio. I was looking at a mountain without a plan for how to get to the
top. I felt stuck in a job I didn't love, and the distance
between my reality and my dream of becoming a broadcaster seemed insurmountable. But as soon as I realized
no one was going to just hand me a radio show, I knew
the first step was up to me. So I started brainstorming
ways to get closer to my dream.

THE PROXIMITY PRINCIPLE

In the introduction, I said that finding opportunities to
do what you love is as simple as getting around the right
people and being in the right *places*. That's The Proximity
Principle. In order to do what you want to do, you have
to be around people who are doing it, in places where
it's happening. My first step, then, was to think about
the personal connections I already had in the broadcasting industry. I'd recently heard about a new cutting-edge
thing called podcasting, and I was eager to try it out.
This was back when iPods had just hit the market. Very
few companies had even heard the term *podcasting*, and
they certainly weren't putting money into it. I knew I was
pretty good on a mic, and starting a podcast was the perfect entry point into a radio show. So I went to a leadership training company in Georgia called Catalyst. Why?
Because I already knew some of the people who worked

there. I was using some of the relationships I had already developed to try to get my foot in the door. I told these folks about this new thing called *podcasting*—and even cut out an article from a technology magazine to show them that it was a real thing!

Because the guys at Catalyst knew and trusted me, they realized there was very little risk involved for them and possibly some potential upside, so they allowed me to launch a podcast. Now this is where it gets good: the *place*. The only space they had available for me to record in was a five foot by five foot sound booth in a warehouse.

> IN ORDER TO DO WHAT YOU WANT TO DO, YOU HAVE TO BE AROUND PEOPLE WHO ARE DOING IT, IN PLACES WHERE IT'S HAPPENING.

And I'm being generous when I say "sound booth." You would almost have to see it to believe it. It didn't even have air conditioning. Have you ever experienced a summer in Georgia? Let me tell you, the humidity and heat take your breath away the second you walk outside. But that didn't matter to me because being in that sound booth—no matter how small and stuffy—meant I was on the right path.

Practicing The Proximity Principle

When I moved into that cramped sound booth, I was nervous and excited. I was also short on equipment, expertise, and experience. But I had created my own broadcasting opportunity, and I believed it would work. It did, but it wasn't as glamorous as I had envisioned. I sat down in front of the mic to record my first leadership podcast, and with each word I spoke, my breath pumped that tiny room with heat. I wish I was joking. Within five minutes I was drenched in sweat! It certainly didn't feel like I had landed my dream job, but I knew it was a start.

I wince when I think back on those podcasts today. It's embarrassing! I had no idea what I was doing, yet somehow—I guess because it was one of the first leadership podcasts out there—I actually had a few listeners. But here's what's more important: that sound booth gave me a chance to do something I was passionate about and gain some real experience in the field I was pursuing. That's what proximity will do for you.

My start-up podcast may not have been at the top of the charts, but as my talent and passion began to intersect, the guys at Catalyst took notice and gave me the chance to emcee their live leadership events. I was so grateful for this opportunity, but, man, I felt like a hot dog in a steak house! I got to interview the famous football coach Tony Dungy and the creator of *Survivor* and *The Voice*, Mark Burnett. I even got to interview a guy who hosted one of the biggest radio shows in America, *The Dave Ramsey Show*.

Without even knowing it, The Proximity Principle was beginning to work in my own journey. Step by step,

I began putting myself in proximity to the right people in the right places. And each step of the way, I was getting in closer proximity to my dream job. Yes, that tiny sound booth

THE BEAUTIFUL THING ABOUT THE PROXIMITY PRINCIPLE IS THAT IT WORKS.

was a humble start. I couldn't always see the significance of what I was doing, and I definitely wasn't doing it well. But it was exactly where I needed to be. I was learning from people who knew what I needed to know. I was working toward my goal and taking another step up the mountain.

I was practicing The Proximity Principle.

The Power of The Proximity Principle

The beautiful thing about The Proximity Principle is that it works. And it keeps on working for as long as you work it. If you want a new job, it works. If you want to change careers, it works. Even if you're already working in the right field and you just want to get to the next level, The Proximity Principle works. To put it into practice, you can start by asking yourself two questions:

1. *Who do I need to know?*
2. *Where do I need to be?*

When I asked myself those questions daily on my journey toward a career in broadcasting, I began to see quick results.

This same principle will work for you too.

Answering those two questions determines your next step. It will help you gain the education, experience, and relationships you need to climb your Mount Everest. You'll never stop growing and improving with this principle in play.

Ready? Let's start climbing!

PART 1

THE PEOPLE

*I feel really grateful to the people who
encouraged me and helped me develop.
Nobody can succeed on their own.*

—SHERYL SANDBERG

The Proximity Principle works. Every. Single. Time. It's not magic. It's a discipline that yields results.

The right people + The right places =
Opportunities.

If you focus on putting this principle to work, you will get closer to your dream job. You can count on it. So where do we start? Let's start with the first part of the equation: people. Because the truth is, it's not just *what* you know; it's *who* you know.

PROXIMITY TO THE RIGHT PEOPLE

People who can help you land your dream job are working hard at this very moment. But they're working for themselves, not for you. In fact, they aren't even thinking about you. They're living their own lives, focusing on their own jobs.

Your job, then, is to get strategic and *find them.*

Finding people who can make opportunities happen for you is the easy part. The hard part is getting some of their time and convincing them to help you on your journey. It's not impossible, but it will take some perseverance and patience. Be prepared for this reality. There will be times when you don't get a response, when you're overlooked, and when you get rejected. Stay with it. Turn that rejection into redirection. Don't let the no's stop you. Instead, let them lead you to the next yes.

Getting a Yes

Here's the deal: to get a yes, don't be an opportunistic jerk. If you approach people with your hand held out for favors like a kid at trick or treat, people will see you coming a mile away and slam the door in your face. If you want people to help you, you need to be the kind of person people want to help. People are more willing to take time out of their day to teach you when you are enthusiastic about learning. My friend Joy talked to me about this.

Joy works in the book publishing world and said, "I love my job, but at times it feels like everyone wants something from me: literary agents, authors, team members. When I'm approached by someone hungry to learn more about the publishing business, it usually stops me in my tracks. It reminds me of how much I love my job, and it gives me a chance to give back." Don't underestimate how your passion to learn and grow can inspire and give life to those around you!

Remember when I contacted the folks at Catalyst about doing a podcast? I didn't just ask them to help me get started in broadcasting. If I had, they would have had nothing to gain, and I would have looked self-serving. Instead, I had to find a way to help them while getting some experience in the process. I approached them with a podcast idea that I believed would benefit them, while giving me some much-needed studio time. It was a win-win for both of us. As you look to others for help, you must approach them with an attitude of gratitude and humility rather than just focusing on gaining something for yourself. You want to develop real relationships with real people. Look for people you can both *give help to* and *get help from.*

GETTING HELP FROM OTHERS IS ESSENTIAL TO YOUR JOURNEY.

Getting help from others is essential to your journey. Climbing a mountain is no easy task, and knowing you're not climbing it alone will help you conquer the mental challenges you'll face. I like to call these mental challenges "limiting beliefs."

LIMITING BELIEFS

The first step in overcoming the limiting beliefs that are holding you back is to identify them. On the path to your dream job, there are two major limiting beliefs that stand in your way: *pride* and *fear.* Let's take a closer look at these and talk about how to recognize these lies.

Pride

Pride shows up in the lie that we are self-sufficient. That we don't need others. That it's weak to rely on others for help and guidance. It also shows up in worrying about how others perceive us. Ironically, pride keeps us from being ambitious. It'd be ridiculous if it wasn't so powerful.

Take Steve Jobs, for instance. Imagine Jobs without ambition. It's impossible, right? I mean, you can't create the iPhone and build a multibillion dollar company without just a little ambition. Arguably, Jobs was one of the most innovative and successful people on the planet. But he didn't get there by being self-sufficient. No, he took a much different approach. At an early age, Jobs learned the value of asking for help. When he was just twelve years old, Jobs called up Bill Hewlett—yep, the Hewlett-Packard co-founder—

> **PRIDE KEEPS US FROM BEING AMBITIOUS.**

to ask for spare parts for a project he was working on. And Bill said yes. To a twelve-year-old kid!

It seems that pride never stopped Jobs from reaching out to others. In a 1994 interview, he talked about the power of asking for help: "I've never found anyone who's said no or hung up the phone when I called—I just asked. And when people ask me, I try to be as responsive, to pay that debt of gratitude back. Most people never pick up the phone and call. Most people never ask. And that's what separates, sometimes, the people that do things from the people that just dream about them."[4]

Setting aside our pride and admitting we need help from others is so critical on the journey to our dream job.

And if someone like Steve Jobs can do it, I'm pretty sure we can too.

Fear

Now let's take a look at the second limiting belief—fear. Fear is normal. There are two kinds of fear that limit us: the *fear of rejection* and the *fear of failure*. Both are liars.

The Fear of Rejection

If you've ever had an idea shot down, you've experienced the sting of rejection. Being told no to a project idea after pouring your heart into the proposal can suck the life right out of you. But the word *no* is not the enemy. Not asking is the enemy. Don't let the fear of rejection keep you from asking. And if you get a no the first time, don't give up. Sometimes you have to get through some hard no's to get to a yes.

> SOMETIMES YOU HAVE TO GET THROUGH SOME HARD NO'S TO GET TO A YES.

Take Patrick. Patrick was an accountant. He had two passions and accounting was not one of them. Patrick enjoyed brewing his own beer, and he loved mission work in Africa. Patrick also had a big imagination. He dreamed of turning beer into water. Okay, technically he wanted to open his own craft brewery as a way to raise money to build fresh water wells in impoverished villages in Africa. And to do this, he needed to learn the craft brewery business from the ground up.

He began by building relationships with local professionals who knew the brewery business. Then he offered a win-win—he would work for free at their brewery if they would teach him the tricks of the trade. Free labor sounds like a no-brainer, right? Apparently not. The first sixteen breweries he approached told him no! But after sixteen no's, the seventeenth said yes, and Patrick spent over a year working for free, even on Saturdays and Sundays. As a result of his efforts, he was able to learn the business—everything from the actual brewing and marketing to packaging and shipping the product. If Patrick had let his fear of rejection keep him from continuing to ask for help, he would have missed out on an unbelievable learning experience. He also wouldn't be where he is today, brewing beer full time. He is doing quite well, and his charity efforts have changed some villages in Africa for generations.

The Fear of Failure

The second kind of fear that limits us is a fear of failure. This often starts with the question: "What if?" *What if someone gives me a shot and I fail?* Sure, failure is a risk. It's part of the deal. But when you know what your top talents, strengths, and skills are, it's absurd to let a limiting belief override the truth that you have what it takes. Remember this: whatever you focus on, you will feel. So don't focus on the possibility of failure. Focus on the truth that you can make this happen. You absolutely have to believe that!

"What if" usually leads to another question: *What will people think?* It would be easy for me just to say, "Who cares what people think!" But the fear of failure can be so acute and personal that we can't help but care. When I was auditioning for TV hosting roles, I got rejection after rejection. I'd go to each audition, hopeful this would be the one where they'd say yes. I'd ask my friends and family to pray for me. Then the sting of rejection would come. I finally stopped asking for prayer because I was embarrassed to report back that I hadn't gotten the gig. It was humiliating and defeating. But deep down I knew that these small failures were not catastrophic. Every audition was a little more practice for the next—all preparing me for the job I really wanted.

The trick is to reframe the way we think about failure. Often, success happens not *despite* failure, but *because* of failure. Thomas Edison had failed inventions. Marie Curie's failures in the lab led to two Nobel Prizes. Albert Einstein had failed equations before the theory of relativity. The list goes on and on. I'd go so far as to say that you can't succeed *unless* and *until* you fail. Failure is what helps us learn and grow, so we shouldn't let our fear of it keep us from trying.

Hockey Hall-of-Famer Wayne Gretzky said it best: "You miss 100% of the shots you don't take." Gretzky knew that in order to score, you have to actually shoot. Did

Gretzky miss some shots? Absolutely. But the fear of missing goals didn't keep him from shooting. Gretzky made 894 career goals, becoming one of the greatest hockey players of all time.[5] He didn't give up when he missed or when they lost a game. He just kept taking shots.

And then there's Will Ferrell, one of the most successful comedic actors in the business. Looking at his career, you might think he is fearless. Not true. He shared his thoughts on the fear of failure in a 2017 commencement speech at the University of Southern California. Ferrell said, "You're never not afraid. . . . But my fear of failure never approached in magnitude my fear of 'what if.' What if I never tried at all?"[6] No matter how high you climb

> OFTEN, SUCCESS HAPPENS NOT *DESPITE* FAILURE, BUT *BECAUSE* OF FAILURE.

or how successful you get, the fear of failure will always threaten to stop your progress. Don't let it! The only way you'll reach your goals is by pushing through the fear, by taking the shot, and by always, *always* choosing to try.

DREAM BIG

Taking the shot isn't always easy. Pride and fear have no shame, and they will try to convince you that your goal is crazy. When I decided to give my dream a shot, I discovered how quickly self-doubt can creep in. I found it difficult to tell my friends and family about my plan because I was worried about what they'd think of me. At the time, I was running a business, and the industry I wanted to move into was such a dramatic change from what I'd been doing. It was a completely different career trajectory. I began to question myself. *Will they think I'm crazy?* I had to learn to call that for what it was: pride.

As I began to put my plan into action, I worried about being told no. I wanted everyone to believe in me and my dream. I wanted to impress everyone and show them I could do this. But that nagging question would pop up. *What if they say no?* I had to learn to call that for what it was: fear of rejection.

> ALL DREAMS ARE A LITTLE CRAZY. THAT'S WHY THEY ARE CALLED "DREAMS."

When I started my climb, I was running my small business and had a wife and three young children counting on me. The possible financial consequences scared me to death. I worried that I'd mess up so bad that I'd destroy my family. *What if I don't have what it takes?* I had to learn to call that for what it was: fear of failure.

The truth is that all dreams are a little crazy. That's why they are called "dreams." But we are never crazy for dreaming. What's crazier than dreaming is never trying at all.

My path began with a start-up podcast in a warehouse closet sound booth with only a handful of people listening. That put me in proximity to the people and the places that allowed me to learn and grow. As I mentioned earlier, one of those people was none other than Dave Ramsey. That podcast interview, although I didn't know it at the time, was the first step that got me where I am today.

The journey to climb your own personal Mount Everest will be wildly different than mine. You'll have your own battles with pride and fear. But don't let the size of the mountain paralyze you. Put one foot in front of the other, up the mountain. You'll reach the top before you know it. Your arrival at the summit will be unique. There is no perfect path. There's only *yours*. So, dream big, ask for help, embrace failure, take the shot, and continue to climb one step at a time.

The People to Look for

As you begin your climb, there are five specific types of people who can help you along the way:

1. **Professors** instruct in the field you want to work in.
2. **Professionals** are the best of the best in their field.
3. **Mentors** offer guidance and accountability.
4. **Peers** accompany you on your journey.

5. **Producers** create jobs, hire and build teams, and
   generate opportunities.

Let's dig in to each of these groups so you'll know
exactly *who* you're looking for, *where* to find them, and
why you need them on your climb.

CHAPTER 2

THE PROFESSORS

*Develop a passion for learning. If you
do, you will never cease to grow.*

—ANTHONY J. D'ANGELO

Tom Petty, legendary musician, songwriter, and member of the Rock & Roll Hall of Fame, had an unbelievable music career and sold over eighty million records during his life. Much of his success can be traced back to the day he met an amazing guitar teacher working in a music store in Gainesville, Florida. That teacher taught Petty pretty much everything he knew about guitar, but that's not all. He also helped Petty develop his trademark sound. Now get this: that teacher's name was Don Felder, a guy so musically gifted that he spent more than twenty-five years as the lead guitarist for another famous band that has sold 150 million records. Maybe you've heard of the Eagles.[7]

Okay, so maybe you don't want to be a legendary musician. That's not the point. The point is: no matter what work you're passionate about, you've got to find the Don Felders to teach you how to do it.

> A PROFESSOR IS SIMPLY A TEACHER— SOMEONE WITH THE SKILLS AND EXPERIENCE IN THE FIELD YOU WANT TO WORK IN.

I like to call these teachers *professors*. What image comes to mind when you hear that word? Do you picture a college professor wearing a tweed jacket with patches on the sleeves? I'm using the word more loosely than that. A professor is simply a teacher—someone with the skills and experience in the field you want to work in.

KEY QUALITIES OF PROFESSORS

So what distinguishes the really good professors from the just-okay ones? I believe that there are three key qualities that make up great professors:

1. They Are Knowledgeable
2. They Are Passionate
3. They Push You to Grow

Great Professors Are Knowledgeable

Professors are key to The Proximity Principle because they have the knowledge base that you need to get started. They have the right certifications or qualifications, whether that means letters after their name or simply someone whose primary job is to teach or train others. The best professors are able to take complex subject matter and break it down in a simple way that's easy to understand.

Great Professors Are Passionate

Professors shouldn't just know their stuff, they should also love sharing their knowledge with others. We've all had professors or teachers at some point in our lives who seemed absolutely miserable. They were grouchy, impatient, and didn't make learning fun for anyone. Great professors don't see what they do as a J-O-B, but as a passion. Their eyes light up when they are sharing all they know, and they truly inspire you to learn from them.

Great Professors Push You to Grow

The best professors can also evaluate your skill level and challenge you to be better, pushing you and forcing you to raise your game. So when you are looking for professors, make sure you find ones who aren't afraid to nudge you out of your comfort zone.

Jessica had a professor like that. I talked to her on *The Ken Coleman Show*, and she explained that while she was taking classes in programming, one of her teachers noticed her talent for building applications and her eye for good design. That professor encouraged Jessica to develop those skills further. When she first started out in programming, she had a specific career path planned, but by the time she graduated, she was a top-level mobile applications developer. That meant she was able to choose the job she wanted! Jessica gave her teacher all the credit for helping her identify her strengths and challenging her to do more than she thought she could. Finding a professor who can push you to your potential like Jessica did is key!

LIFELONG LEARNER

Regardless of how great the professors are in your life, the responsibility to learn begins and ends with you. You must never stop learning, no matter how high you climb. Award-winning actress Viola Davis is a great example of someone who understands the importance of learning.

Davis has been nominated for three Academy Awards and has achieved the Triple Crown of Acting, which means she has received an Oscar, an Emmy, and a Tony. Why? What was the secret that made Viola Davis so successful? Was it raw talent? Luck? No, Davis began her acting career with an intense desire to learn. She positioned herself to study under professors at The Juilliard School. In a 2013 interview, Davis spoke proudly of her education: "The reason why I went to Juilliard, the reason why I got a degree in acting, is that I wanted people to understand that I could be technically proficient as an actor, that I'm not just up there flying by the seat of my pants."[8]

> YOU MUST NEVER STOP LEARNING, NO MATTER HOW HIGH YOU CLIMB.

In another interview, Davis commented that she still maintains communication with her acting instructors and stays open to learning new skills and techniques.[9] That respect and gratitude for her professors—even after earning acclaim and success—distinguishes her as a true star who understands that to excel in your craft you must always be learning.

So what's the takeaway here? Like Viola Davis, you must look for opportunities to find professors who will invest in you every step along the way. Again, no one is sitting around thinking about how they can help you find your dream job. Even the best professors aren't going to seek you out. It's your job to seek them out and stay connected with them as you climb—and sometimes even after you climb—the mountain.

BACK TO THE BASICS

Who was that great professor in my own journey? I knew that what I needed was basic knowledge and skills about the broadcasting industry. So I spent some time researching around the Atlanta area until I found a broadcasting school run by a local television producer named Jeff Batten. I called Jeff and asked if he would be willing to meet with me at his office. Within moments of talking to him, I realized that he was an expert and that his class was exactly what I needed from an educational standpoint.

> NO ONE IS SITTING AROUND THINKING ABOUT HOW THEY CAN HELP YOU FIND YOUR DREAM JOB.

I'll never forget that first night of class. I was in my early thirties, about a decade older than everybody else in the class, and most certainly the only guy there with a wife, three kids, and a mortgage. I can still remember the confused looks on several of the students' faces when they realized I wasn't the instructor. Talk about a humbling experience! It actually took a couple of weeks for my classmates to stop calling me "sir!"

It's funny to look back on it now, but in the moment, I didn't care that I was the oldest student in the class. I was having fun! I wanted to be there because I was hungry to learn anything and everything that would get me in proximity of my dream job. So hungry that I was willing to look like the odd man out just so I could learn from Jeff. His knowledge was invaluable to me. Having worked in the broadcasting industry, he knew all of the latest trends and approaches to the craft. His class is where I learned some of the basics that I still use today—things like how to use a microphone well, how to edit audio and video, and how to do a news report for television and radio. He taught me the fundamentals of broadcasting, gave me practical experience, and sent me on my way with a lot more confidence than when I started.

I was really lucky to learn from Jeff, and I will forever be grateful to him for sharing his knowledge with me. Yet, while his teaching greatly impacted my career, it was *my* responsibility to put what I learned into practice.

That's your responsibility too. As you pursue proximity to your dream job, look for professors who will take the time to teach you, respect the knowledge they share and incorporate it into your work. Commit to being a lifelong learner!

THE PROXIMITY PROCESS

1. Review the key qualities of great professors at the start of this chapter.

2. Research what you need to learn to be qualified for your "Mount Everest" dream job.

3. Determine which people are good at teaching what you need to learn, then make a list of the classes or opportunities available both locally and nationally.

CHAPTER 3

THE PROFESSIONALS

*[Professionals] possess a mastery
mentality—with the goal of
becoming the best they can be.*

—KEVIN EIKENBERRY

Have you ever heard the phrase "talent imitates; genius steals"? T. S. Eliot, the great American writer and poet, gets credit for that one. Imitating the work of others is really just a way to practice the skills and techniques that others have mastered. It's when you master their work then make it your own that the "genius" kicks in.

Robin Williams was a comic genius. A versatile, vibrant actor and comedian, Williams was a four-time Academy Award nominee. He won the Oscar for his performance in *Good Will Hunting* and was given several other awards, including four Grammys. He was the best of the best, a true professional in his field.

So how did Williams become the best? Growing up, he often watched *The Tonight Show* and was captivated by the entertainers. He used a tape recorder to capture audio of the comedians who appeared on the show and would spend the next day listening to those recordings over and over, memorizing the jokes and matching the timing of the punch lines.[10] Because he loved comedy, he practiced it long before he took the stage himself.

Robin Williams is considered a genius not because he could tell other people's jokes, but because he found an approach distinctly his own. That is exactly the mind-set you need when you watch the professionals in your industry. Study what makes them the best. Imitate it. Then make it your own.

KEY QUALITIES OF PROFESSIONALS

To get in proximity to your dream job, you need to find professionals who are excelling at the work you'd love to do at the highest level. Professionals have key qualities that make them the best at what they do:

1. They Are Experienced
2. They Study Other Professionals

Now let's dig into both of these qualities a little more.

Professionals Are Experienced

As you begin to look for professionals, you should find people who are at least ten years ahead of you in your career. There is no substitute for experience, and they have it—and all the wisdom that goes with it! Let's go back to the idea of climbing your personal Mount Everest. You could think of professionals as the accomplished mountaineers who have expertly navigated the summit—people like Sir Edmund Hillary.

> TO GET IN PROXIMITY TO YOUR DREAM JOB, YOU NEED TO FIND PROFESSIONALS WHO ARE EXCELLING AT THE WORK YOU'D LOVE TO DO AT THE HIGHEST LEVEL.

In 1953 Hillary was one of just two mountaineers who were the first to actually climb to the top of Mount Everest. The following year he and four others became the first to successfully take vehicles to the South Pole. Then over thirty years later, Hillary and Neil Armstrong flew to the North Pole in a small plane, making Hillary the first person ever to reach the summit of Mount Everest and trek to both the North and South Poles.[11] Now that's a guy I'd want to have by my side when I was climbing a mountain. He was an expert in his field and was driven to succeed! Hillary's determination and willingness to push past his comfort level was what got him to the top of Mount Everest, and those same qualities will help you reach your own goals.

Professionals Study Other Professionals

Professionals also spend time studying other professionals they admire and look up to. Academy Award winning actor Leonardo DiCaprio was influenced by the legendary leading man Paul Newman.[12] Filmmaker M. Night Shyamalan grew up learning from the work of his own favorite filmmaker, Steven Spielberg.[13] Even The Beatles, arguably the most famous band in the world, modeled their style after the early work of rock legend Chuck Berry.[14] And while we all aren't famous actors, filmmakers, or musicians, we can find people who are top-notch professionals in the field we want to be in and we can imitate them. Find professionals working in proximity to your Mount Everest—the ones who are at the top of their game. These are the people who can show you the tricks of the trade and give you insight into what it takes to succeed.

That's The Proximity Principle at work!

LEARNING FROM PROFESSIONALS

As an aspiring broadcaster, I had a lot to learn about the art of interviewing. I wanted to learn from the greats who'd inspired me, like Larry King, Bob Costas, and David Frost.

I knew it was unlikely that I'd have the opportunity to sit down with them, but there was so much I wanted to learn. So I did my research.

I spent hours on the internet watching Larry King, learning his approach—how he allowed a certain silence after he posed a question and how his demeanor affected his guests. I paid attention to how Bob Costas was engaged and present but always poised to ask the perfect follow-up question. I studied David Frost's zingers and distinctive personality. By watching and studying them, I was able to try on various approaches. I borrowed their tools and tactics. And I gained a wealth of wisdom through the work I put in.

Watching professionals on the internet or on television is a useful tactic, but you can't stop there. You need to go deeper, and that means finding a few professionals to talk to and learn from face-to-face. Emmy Award-winning broadcaster Ernie Johnson of TNT was one of the first professional broadcasters I got to sit down with. I'd seen Ernie do interviews on TV and admired how effortlessly he navigated the set with huge personalities like Charles Barkley, Kenny Smith, and Shaquille O'Neal. Ernie is somehow able to put these guys at ease, and he seems to be having so much fun with them that you forget he's actually working! I wanted to be able to imitate that skill. So when I had the opportunity to interview him for a leadership podcast, I jumped at the chance. And the cool thing is, we went to the same church and had a mutual friend. So I used that connection to ask for a personal visit with him. I knew there was a risk that he'd say no, but it was a risk I just had to take. I would've kicked myself if I didn't at least try! And it worked! I was able to get a couple of meetings with him and hear his story.

As I spent time with Ernie, I learned that it's the hard work he does behind the scenes that allows him to be so spontaneous live. Before he takes his seat on the set, he does a ton of preparation and research. He pours over players' statistics and storylines in relation to the teams that are matching up that night. He arrives on set at about one o'clock in the afternoon, shortly after lunch, and he's there until after midnight most nights.

IT TAKES A LOT OF HARD WORK TO APPEAR EFFORTLESS.

Ernie Johnson helped me understand that it takes a lot of hard work to appear effortless. My short time speaking with him showed me how his preparation was the source of his confidence. Hearing about the sacrifices he made— the late nights and the time away from his family—and the countless hours he put in to become one of the most talented sports broadcasters in America was fascinating. And it gave me incredible energy.

Preparing for the Pros

When you have the opportunity to spend time with pros—whether a celebrity or a local business person—it's important to follow Ernie's example and arrive prepared. This isn't just a matter of maximizing your time with that person so you get the most out of the conversation. It's a matter of respect. These professionals are giving their time, probably one of their most valuable resources. Honoring their *time* is a great way to honor *them*.

I love the story my friend Brad tells about his development as a head coach. After he was hired in his first job, he began to look around at the other successful coaches in his city. He called Coach Reynolds, who'd won three state titles, and asked him if he could visit. Coach Reynolds agreed, but he told Brad he only had a half hour before practice to talk, so Brad arrived promptly, showing up prepared with well-researched and focused questions. Brad even kept a timer on his phone to be sure he didn't take up more than the allotted thirty minutes. Coach Reynolds was so impressed with Brad's respect, timeliness, and hunger to learn that he invited Brad back to watch several practices! Brad says the strategies he absorbed as a young coach from top-level professionals like Coach Reynolds have made an invaluable impact on his success.

This is the same mind-set you need to have when you approach professionals. Just like Brad, show up prepared and be respectful, proving that you mean business and want to be intentional. With that mind-set, you'll get so many more opportunities to learn from the best in your field. And there's always a lot to learn!

Steps to Learning from the Pros

You have to *learn* from the best of the best in order to *become* one of the best. When learning from professionals, you want to focus on doing three things:

1. Learn Their Tricks of the Trade
2. Develop Your Own Method
3. Understand that Wisdom Comes from Experience

Let's dive a little deeper into these three key areas.

Learn Their Tricks of the Trade

The first thing you'll want to focus on when studying the pros is their tricks of the trade. By this, I mean the actual skills, hacks, and techniques that keep professionals at the top. As a basketball fan, I was always fascinated by Kobe Bryant's approach to the game. His dad had been a professional basketball player, and Kobe grew up relentlessly studying game film. Even as a young kid, he didn't just watch the professionals of his era, he studied old tapes of the greatest players in basketball history. Kobe would pick up different tricks from each one. He copied Oscar Robertson's hesitation moves, modeled Elgin Baylor's footwork, and practiced Jerry West's quick-

> YOU HAVE TO *LEARN* FROM THE BEST OF THE BEST IN ORDER TO *BECOME* ONE OF THE BEST.

shooting release. Later, as a high school player, he tested these tools out during his games. Kobe Bryant, the player who would later score eighty-one points in a professional game and who is considered one of the greatest NBA players of all time, was dedicated to studying the professionals in the game of basketball and integrating their techniques into his own game.[15]

Develop Your Own Method

Remember, when studying the pros, the goal is not to imitate exactly how they do things. Your job is to watch and learn what methods they used to help them succeed, then make them your own.

Take Ryan, for instance. Ryan was learning the ropes of a new sales job in logistics and was determined to learn from the best. He sought out the top performers in his company and asked if he could spend a day making sales calls with each of them. A couple of them agreed.

Ryan first flew to the Midwest to spend a day with Mike, a sales pro who was gregarious, funny, loud, and full of personality. When I say "full of personality," I mean Mike would visit clients on Halloween wearing a costume! But Mike was also the type of sales representative who knew the names of his clients' spouses and children and was focused on spending quality time with people, even if it put him a little behind schedule. Ryan took extensive notes during the sales call, then flew home eager to learn even more from the next professional that had agreed to let him tag along. He drove south and went on a few calls with Claire, another high-achieving sales representative in his company. Claire's approach was completely different from Mike's. Claire was particular, efficient, and businesslike in all of her calls. While she didn't seem to have the same type of personal relationship with her clients, she was polite, well received, and it was clear her clients had full confidence in her. Ryan couldn't imagine Claire dressing up for Halloween, but her approach was just as effective.

These two high achievers couldn't have been more different! When he got home, Ryan got to work "trying on" the different methods he learned from Mike and Claire. But imitating their style was not the way to go. He had to find a way to interact with his clients that worked best for him. Because of the time he spent observing both of these highly successful professionals in his field, Ryan had a baseline of successful methods to model and make his own.

There are a variety of ways to work in your field and be successful. Some people work best when decked out in a power suit while others work better in jeans (or even a Halloween costume). Studying the pros will help you come up with what's best for you.

Understand that Wisdom Comes from Experience

Wisdom is only gained through experience. When you sit down to learn from professionals, pay close attention to their stories. Listen to how they got to the top and don't overlook their struggles. Remember, there's no perfect path. You can gain a lot of wisdom from the setbacks and challenges professionals have faced on their climb. Vernon Law said, "Experience is a hard teacher because she gives the test first, the lesson afterward." Every professional has learned a few lessons the hard way. Here are a few questions to keep in mind as you dig into their stories:

> YOU CAN GAIN A LOT OF WISDOM FROM THE SETBACKS PROFESSIONALS HAVE FACED ON THEIR CLIMB.

1. How did they get to their dream job?
2. How did they earn their reputation?
3. What strategic choices did they make?
4. How did they handle disappointment?
5. What did they do when they failed?
6. How did they overcome the fear of failure and rejection?
7. Who did they learn from?
8. How long did it take them to reach their goal or get the position they wanted?

One fascinating example of how studying other professionals can pay off in a big way comes from a CEO who turned his shareholder meetings into dramatic showcases for new products. He staged huge, drama-filled events that often had live music and slides to demonstrate his cutting-edge products. That description probably had you thinking of the founder of Apple, Steve Jobs. If so, you're wrong! Ever heard of Edwin Land? Land, a brilliant scientist, inventor, and the co-founder of Polaroid, was the architect of this type of technological showmanship in the late 1960s. He was also eventually fired from the very company he started and never quite got his career back on track.

Steve Jobs learned so much from Edwin Land and credited him as one who inspired him to greatness. Jobs modeled his Apple product events after Land's famous Polaroid meetings, and when Apple let Jobs go in the mid-1980s, he was able to learn from the failures in Land's story and apply them to his own comeback. Jobs later returned to Apple and grew the company to unprecedented heights. Because of Jobs's careful study of successful professionals like Land, he was able to truly become the best in his field.[16]

And this is how you will become the best in your field—by studying other professionals who have a wealth of wisdom and experience, learning from their skills and techniques, and making them your own. These are the accomplished mountain climbers, the ones who have expertly navigated their own mountains, and learning from their setbacks and challenges will help you push through difficult times and inspire you to climb higher.

THE PROXIMITY PROCESS

1. Research the pros who excel in your field.

2. Decide which pros you'd like to connect with, then schedule a meeting and prepare for it by reviewing the sample questions in the "Understand that Wisdom Comes from Experience" section of this chapter.

3. Identify alternative ways to learn from the pros you can't meet with in person.

CHAPTER 4

THE MENTORS

I don't care what you do for a living—if you do it well, I'm sure there was someone cheering you on or showing the way. A mentor.

—DENZEL WASHINGTON

Early in my career there was a moment when I desperately needed some guidance and encouragement. I pulled into my driveway one evening after work feeling completely down because several major opportunities had fallen through. I had been working incredibly hard, but I didn't feel like I was making any progress toward my goals. I knew I needed to pull myself together before I went into the house to greet my wife and kids, so I picked up the phone to call my mentor, Don.

Don answered my call, and he listened. He didn't ridicule me. He didn't tell me to stop expecting everything to fall perfectly into place. He gave me a piece of advice: "Ken, sometimes the best thing we can do is to be patient as we press forward." He was able to cut right to the truth and tell me I wasn't seeing the big picture, giving me the perspective I needed. Don was able to speak into my situation because he had experienced it in his own life. He continues to be a trusted guide for me, and his impact on my life and career is evident to me every day.

THE POWER OF A MENTOR

Pick up the biography of almost any successful person, and you'll find that their accomplishments were supported by a mentor. Mentors are people who can guide, encourage, and hold you accountable as you make the climb to your dream job. The reality is that over 80 percent of American CEOs have have had a mentor.[17] In fact, many of the world's most recognizable and influential people attribute much of their success to the counsel of a mentor. Here are just a few of those examples:

> MENTORS ARE PEOPLE WHO CAN GUIDE, ENCOURAGE, AND HOLD YOU ACCOUNTABLE AS YOU MAKE THE CLIMB TO YOUR DREAM JOB.

48

- Media mogul Oprah Winfrey once explained, "A mentor is someone who allows you to see the hope inside yourself." Winfrey was mentored by the renowned American poet Maya Angelou.
- Facebook CEO Mark Zuckerberg sought out the late Steve Jobs, founder and CEO of Apple, to be his mentor.
- Dr. Martin Luther King Jr. was mentored by Benjamin Mays, the president of Morehouse College.[18]

My guess is you've already noticed the power of the mentor relationship. It's reflected over and over in some of our favorite movies. Luke Skywalker couldn't have defeated the Empire without Obi-Wan Kenobi; the Karate Kid needed Mr. Miyagi to help him win; Harry Potter needed Dumbledore to give him insight; and Katniss Everdeen wouldn't have won the Hunger Games without Haymitch. Just like these movie heroes, we need a trustworthy guide to help us on our own journey. The right mentor can make a huge difference in getting you in closer proximity to a job you love.

KEY QUALITIES OF A MENTOR

So who are these people? What gives mentors the unique ability to help others stay grounded yet grow? And how are they able to guide and direct people in a lasting and meaningful way? In my experience, there are three key qualities that make up every great mentor.

1. They Are Accomplished
2. They Are Understanding
3. They Are Caring

I can say for certain that my own mentor has these qualities, and the mentors in your own life should have them too.

Mentors Are Accomplished

Mentors are people who are accomplished in an area of life or work where you would like guidance. Sometimes that area is work, but it could also be parenting, leadership, or just life in general. These are people you can look to for support and learn from the wisdom they've gained along the way. You may respect them for the way they raise their kids or serve the community. Maybe they are a hard worker or have reached a level of leadership in their company that you aspire to. No matter what accomplishments you admire them for, mentors understand how to climb the mountain you want to climb, because they've climbed a few of their own.

Mentors Are Understanding

The best mentors have faced their share of obstacles and understand the big picture of how to navigate hardships. Mentors demonstrate the experience, knowledge, and good judgment that only comes from the wisdom of having "been there and done that." They are often empathetic because they've failed, picked themselves back up, and tried again. They know what it feels like to be afraid, but they have enough life experience to know when you push past the fear, that's when the real magic happens. If they're older, they may see a younger version of themselves in you. They'll share their experiences and wisdom with you because they want to see you win. And more than likely they had their own mentor who did the same for them.

Mentors Are Caring

Finally, you want to find a mentor who's caring, always keeping your best interest in mind. A great mentor understands the deep value of the mentor/mentee relationship, and they are more than willing to help others the way that they have been helped. They won't just tell you what you want to hear. Instead, they will tell you hard truths when

> MENTORS WILL TELL YOU HARD TRUTHS WHEN YOU NEED TO HEAR THEM.

you need to hear them because that's what people who truly care about you will do. They know that this builds trust and is a critical part of being a mentor. Otherwise they'd just be a cheerleader. They practice The Golden

Rule, treating others the way they would want to be treated, and they genuinely and patiently care for others and want to see them grow.

MENTORSHIP AT WORK

Finding the right mentor to help you grow isn't easy. You don't want to rush the process. There's not an Obi-Wan Kenobi around every corner. And even if you do find the right person to mentor you, let go of the idea that learning from them is a silver bullet that will unveil the answers to all of life's questions. It doesn't work that way. A mentor is just one of many people you need on your climb. In fact, the reality is you're likely to have more than one mentor along the way. As your path takes twists and turns, you should seek out multiple mentors to guide you in the different areas and stages of your life. Taking the time to pursue mentor relationships is an important key to your success, because when you strike gold and find one (or several) who is willing to invest in your life, you'll get in closer proximity—not just to *where* you want to be—to *who* you want to be.

So what do you want your career to look like in twenty or thirty years? Now look around. Who do you know, even as a distant acquaintance, whose professional life reflects the qualities that you want for your own? Remember that a mentor doesn't have to work in your specific field or discipline. You can start by looking at your personal network—your family, friends, coworkers, and acquaintances. Then look for people who are a generation ahead of you.

Once you find that person, be bold in asking them to mentor you. Don't let pride or fear get in the way. Good mentors are usually products of good mentors, so they understand the importance of your request and will probably be honored that you asked. Remember, don't rush the process of finding a good one. This may be someone who will be a part of your life for years, so be patient until you find the right person.

Setting Expectations

Like every important relationship, building a strong connection with a mentor takes time and intention. Once you find someone who agrees to mentor you, be clear about what you're asking them to do, and communicate how much you value their time. When Oprah Winfrey was just a young Chicago news anchor, she approached Maya Angelou for the first time. She promised Maya she would only take five minutes of her day. After Oprah finished with her questions, Maya glanced curiously at her watch and noticed it had been exactly five minutes to the second. Maya smiled, paused in admiration, and asked, "Who are you, girl?"[19] That short meeting was the beginning of a lifelong, influential mentorship. And I'm sure Oprah's respect for one of Maya's most valuable resources—her time—played a big part in that.

Practically, you'll want to sit down with your mentor in person and express your desire to grow. You should communicate that they are someone you admire and respect. And your attitude and actions should show a posture of humility and honor. These people have conquered many mountains. You want to learn from their wisdom, and you want to do that with a tremendous amount of respect.

Next, you want to decide how often and for how long you and your mentor will meet. Maybe it's once a quarter at first, and eventually that might lead to meeting once a month. It doesn't have to be a set or regular meeting. It's just important that when you meet, you work around your mentor's schedule and come prepared with an agenda and specific questions. They need to see that this is a good return on their investment of time. This doesn't need to be intense, but it does need to be intentional!

MEETING WITH A MENTOR DOESN'T NEED TO BE INTENSE, BUT IT DOES NEED TO BE INTENTIONAL.

Lance is a great example of someone with a healthy, intentional relationship with his mentor. Lance was managing a successful import business when he began to run into some serious challenges. He couldn't seem to find the right sales person and was struggling to balance work and his marriage. I challenged him to find a mentor he could look to for some wisdom. Through a mutual friend he found Ralph, a guy who just happened to be the president of a successful flooring company. Ralph had a great family life, was very involved in supporting a local homeless shelter, and had many of the characteristics of a life Lance aspired to live. Lance asked Ralph to meet, and soon the two began meeting for lunch once a month. Ralph was able to provide critical guidance for Lance.

As the years passed, Lance's life began to reflect the same level of success as his mentor's. But it didn't happen overnight. This was a long-term investment for both Lance and Ralph. And the same will be true for you. If you treat your own mentor relationships with the same purpose and intention, they can act as rocket fuel for your personal and professional growth.

You Are Never Too Successful to Need a Mentor

Need more evidence of the power of mentorship? Take this example from one of the most recognizable businesspeople in the world, Bill Gates. As co-founder and CEO of Microsoft—and an incredibly influential philanthropist—you'd think someone so successful, so accomplished, and so bright wouldn't need a mentor. But that couldn't be further from the truth. In a 2013 TED Talk, Gates talked about the importance of mentors in his life. "Everyone needs a coach," he said. "It doesn't matter whether you're a basketball player, a tennis player, a gymnast, or a bridge player. We all need people who will give us feedback. That's how we improve."[20]

Bill Gates credits Warren Buffett as having a huge impact on his own life and career. Buffett is one of the world's wealthiest investors, with a net worth of over $80 billion, and he's the CEO of Berkshire Hathaway, a holding company that owns well-known brands such as Duracell, Geico, and Dairy Queen. He's also famous for his commitment to give away 99 percent of his wealth to philanthropy.[21] Buffett's mentorship and coaching of Gates helped him better understand investing, platform building, and the value of his own time.[22] Gates said of his friend, "He has lived by the same principles of integrity and creating business value since day one. He sets a wonderful example, and even though I have known him well for more than twenty-five years, I have never stopped learning from him."[23]

Gates joked that he had no choice but to look up to another one of his mentors, six-foot-seven physician Dr. William Foege, whom he credits for teaching him about public health. Gates said of his mentor, "One of the most valuable contributions Bill made to our learning was giving us a reading list with eighty-one different books and reports on global health issues. All these books opened a new world for me, making Bill's passion for fighting poverty and disease a passion of my own." Dr. Foege's mentorship helped guide the Bill & Melinda Gates Foundation's medical efforts around the world, making them what they are today.[24]

Gates's relationship with these men is further evidence

of the lasting impact mentors can have, no matter where you are on your path to success!

Pass the Torch

The beautiful thing about lasting mentor relationships is that you'll eventually see so much personal growth in your life from the guidance and encouragement you receive that it'll challenge you to mentor others. Think of it like this: you've seen the process of passing the Olympic torch from runner to runner, right? Each runner covers a certain distance and imparts fire to the next runner. That fire is such an appropriate metaphor for the wisdom of mentorship and how it should be passed on.

When you take hold of the wisdom and knowledge you've received from your mentor and pass it on to the next generation, the mentor relationship has come full circle. You only truly realize how much mentors themselves received from helping you when you commit to mentoring others. So when you ask someone to be your mentor, do it with confidence! Then one day, when someone asks *you* to be *their* mentor, jump at the opportunity to pass the torch.

You need mentors to guide you, to encourage you, and to equip you. Often when you have your head down and your nose to the grindstone, working hard to get to where you want to go, it can be hard to see if you are making progress. You need a guide who can see the big picture! Mentors can give you perspective because they have more life and career experience. They have already made many of the mistakes you haven't made yet, and you can learn from their mistakes while navigating your own. If you can commit to listening and learning from them, you'll begin to see the same traits you admire in them taking root in your own life. Then one day you can take all that you've learned from them and from your own experiences and pass it on to others.

THE PROXIMITY PROCESS

1. Think about what you want your career to look like in twenty years, then make a list of people you know whose professional life matches your long-term career goals. Include why you admire them and how you want to be challenged by them or learn from them.

2. Determine what you want to learn from your potential mentor, then decide how often and for how long you would like to meet with them.

3. Schedule an initial meeting to share your desire and expectations with your potential mentor.

CHAPTER 5

THE PEERS

*Don't join an easy crowd; you won't
grow. Go where the expectations and
the demands to perform are high.*

—JIM ROHN

Tim was a successful sales person at a medical company when he decided to commit to a men's fitness group. The group, dubbed *F3* for their commitment to fitness, fellowship, and faith, was made up of highly successful and driven executives. They met three days a week at 5:30 in the morning to run, lift weights, and grab a quick coffee to talk about life. Tim joined the group to get fit and lose a little weight. But he got so much more out of it than that.

As he kept meeting with these guys, Tim began to pick up some of their habits. After one full year in F3, Tim had the highest sales numbers of his career. Several months into his second year in the group, he was promoted to a regional management position. Tim had quickly become an executive-level employee just like the men he worked out with.

Tim credited much of his success to how much time he spent with the goal-oriented guys in his F3 group. The momentum he received from hanging out regularly with other men who were winning professionally pushed him forward. They were striving together and challenging each other to work harder and to be better in the gym and in life.

I love Tim's story because it's a real-life example of the law of averages at work. American entrepreneur, author, and motivational speaker Jim Rohn said that we are the average of the five people we spend the most time around.[25] He based this idea on the law of averages, a theory that suggests the result of any given situation will be the average of all the outcomes. So one way to think of it is: if all of my friends are nines out of tens, I've got a good shot at becoming a nine too. Here's the point: as you're getting in closer proximity to your dream job, you'll climb faster and further by surrounding yourself with people who are focused, driven, and motivated to reach their own goals. To reach the summit you've got to get in proximity of peers who elevate your game.

THE POWER OF STRONG PEERS

Typically, peers are your equals. At work they're your coworkers. At home they're your siblings. They're the people walking alongside you in the same stage of life, pretty close in economic status and age. So with the law of averages in mind, take a look around and ask yourself these questions: *Who am I spending the most time with? Who is challenging and championing me?*

It's pretty common to discover that you're surrounded by environmental peers. These are the people you have a shared history with, like a childhood friend or college buddy. Or the people you frequently bump into in common locations, like your neighbors, the parents of the other kids on a sports team, or a friend at church. There's absolutely nothing wrong with environmental peers. There's a

> YOU'LL CLIMB FASTER AND FURTHER BY SURROUNDING YOURSELF WITH PEOPLE WHO ARE FOCUSED, DRIVEN, AND MOTIVATED TO REACH THEIR OWN GOALS.

place for those people in your life. But there's a difference between environmental peers and intentional peers. That difference is *purpose*. Sometimes environmental peers are comfortable with where they are in life, so they're not in the right mind-set to help you climb your Mount

Everest. Now let me be clear about what I'm *not* saying. I'm not saying being comfortable with where you are in life is a bad thing. Not at all. In fact, it's a good thing. But that's not where *you* are right now. Right now, you are gearing up to climb a mountain, and you need to surround yourself with peers who are climbing their own mountains.

In the 1960s, there was a legendary group of celebrities called the "Rat Pack." This group of peers included big names like Frank Sinatra, Sammy Davis Jr., Dean Martin, Joey Bishop, and Peter Lawford. They starred in the original version of the movie *Ocean's 11* and were also responsible for twenty-some movies and countless famous records. These gentlemen were the marquee names from the early days of film, music, and comedy that led to the true glitz and glamour of American entertainment's pop culture.

Since then other famous friend groups have been given similar nicknames. In the 1980s, a group of young actors, including Emilio Estevez, Anthony Michael Hall, Andrew McCarthy, Demi Moore, Rob Lowe, Ally Sheedy, Judd Nelson, and Molly Ringwald was nicknamed the "Brat Pack." Then in 2004, a group of comedy actors who appeared in some of the hit comedy movies since the mid-nineties was dubbed the "Frat Pack." This group included people like Ben Stiller, Jack Black, Owen Wilson, Luke Wilson, Will Ferrell, and Vince Vaughn.

Here's one more example of peers challenging each

other onscreen as well as in real life. Comedian Adam Sandler is intentional about working on material with fellow comedians Kevin James, David Spade and Chris Rock. In a 2013 interview, Sandler said, "Here's how I think of my scripts. I sit in my room and think up an idea. Then I call up all my friends and they say: 'That's awesome! You are the best.' No, what really happens is that a group of us come up with an idea and work on it."[26] Sandler and his peers take making jokes seriously. They

IF YOU FEEL CHALLENGED, INSPIRED, AND ENCOURAGED AFTER BEING WITH THEM, YOU'VE FOUND THE RIGHT PEERS.

have high expectations of themselves and each other, challenging, inspiring, and pushing each other to be better comedians.

And that's what all of these groups have done for each other. They may have first been thrown together as environmental peers, cast in the same movies. But they soon became intentional peers, refining each other and working hard to be the best at their craft.

So who are the peers in your own life? How do you feel after spending time with them? If you feel challenged, inspired, and encouraged after being with them, you've found the right peers who are driven by intention and purpose.

KEY QUALITIES OF PEERS

As you begin to get intentional about finding the right peers, there are three key qualities you need to look for:

1. They Have Shared Values
2. They Have Drive
3. They Speak Truth

Let's dig into each of these.

Peers Should Have Shared Values

"As iron sharpens iron, so one person sharpens another."[27] This biblical proverb cuts to the chase. Notice that it doesn't say, as *clay* sharpens iron. Iron sharpens iron because the two elements have identical properties. They're made up of the same stuff. In the same way, peers who can sharpen you share your same values.

Let's take a closer look at this. If you want to identify the people who share your values, you've got to clearly define what matters to you. Make a list. Write down the values you practice, admire, and aspire to in your own life—things like honesty, integrity, and hard work. Now think about your peers. Who do you know with the same values? You may find these individuals among people you already know, but if you don't, it's time to broaden your search. Remember, you're working your way up the side of your mountain here, and you need the right people at your side.

Peers Should Have Drive

I recently completed my first half marathon. When I started training, I wanted to see whether or not I was getting faster, so I kept track of my minutes per mile. I quickly saw a huge difference in my times when I was running by myself versus training with others. When I ran on my own, I could get a little slow when I was tired. The self-doubt would start to creep in. I would focus on how miserable I was and how crazy I was for attempting this. Sometimes I'd even cut my training short if I wasn't feeling it. But when I trained with a partner, it added a level of healthy competition that led to a much better pace, and I wasn't tempted to quit. Running with peers who had the same drive to show up, put in the miles, and work hard week after week helped motivate me to practice with that same level of drive—if not more. And this is true in your own climb. Finding peers who set high standards for themselves and commit to do what it takes every day to maintain or exceed those standards will challenge you to keep moving forward too.

Peers Should Speak Truth

The truth hurts, but it can also drive you to be better. The right peers will speak truth to you, even when it's hard, because they want to push you to reach your goals. Finding a peer who will tell you like it is, is a rare quality and you need to hold on to them.

I'll never forget one defining moment early in my broadcasting career that I owe to a longtime friend and peer, Bill Hampton. Bill and I met back in college at a student government assembly. I remember hearing him give a short but impressive talk from the stage. Afterward I walked up to talk to him and introduced myself, and like they say, "the rest is history." We've been friends ever since.

So let me tell you how Bill's ability to speak the truth has impacted my career. I'd just finished one of my Saturday morning radio shows and was driving home feeling pretty good about it. Classic me, I wasn't thinking too much about it—just flying high on a feeling of accomplishment. Then my phone rang. "Ken!" the familiar voice greeted me. "I just listened to your show today, and I have some notes . . ." Those words hung in the air for a second. Bill continued, "To be honest—it was terrible." Bill proceeded to tell me everything I did wrong and how I should fix it. He went on. For ten full minutes.

Now let me first say that there are only a handful of people who care about me enough to be that brutally honest. And you know what? I really appreciated it because I knew he genuinely cared about me and wanted me to improve. Sure, his honesty was hard to hear in the moment, especially after feeling I had done so well, but I needed that hard feedback. I needed to hear the truth. And who else was going to give it to me? Bill understood how badly I wanted a career in broadcasting, and he was always cheering me on and pushing me to get better. I am so thankful for the many ways Bill's friendship has impacted my career, and I take his input very seriously. And although it can sometimes be hard to hear honest feedback from others, you need peers like Bill who are willing to tell you the truth so you can learn and grow.

Here's another example of how honest input from peers can sharpen you. You can't watch an interview with a comedian who came to prominence in the 1970s without hearing stories about a Los Angeles nightclub called The Comedy Store, owned by Mitzi Shore. It was a hot spot that drew many of the most talented young comedians from all over the country. These comedians were environmental peers at first, but they quickly became intentional peers. As they performed at this club, they began hanging out together and eventually formed strong friendships, honing their comedy routines. After shows, the comedians would head up the hill to Mitzi's house, to hang out and cut up with each other late into the night. When I picture this in my head, I imagine these guys rolling with laughter as they practiced new jokes on each other. But they weren't just there for the fun. They critiqued each other's writing and gave input on each other's performances. This peer group produced many of the giants of American comedy, greats such as Jerry Seinfeld, Jay Leno, David Letterman, Dana Carvey, and Robin Williams. To this day, many of these guys stay in close contact with one another.[28]

Connecting with the right peers will accelerate your growth as you learn how other high achievers approach the important areas of life such as work, faith, and family. A strong peer group will give you the encouragement you need to stay focused on your goals when your climb gets tough. They'll challenge your pace and push you to new levels in your journey.

THE PROXIMITY PROCESS

1. Write down the five peers you spend the most time with.

2. Answer the following questions for each of them:

   ▸ Do we share the same values?
   ▸ Do they challenge me to aim higher?
   ▸ Do they give honest feedback?

3. Now write down the five peers that you need to spend more time with based on the key qualities listed in this chapter.

CHAPTER 6

THE PRODUCERS

*I like things to happen; and if they don't
happen, I like to make them happen.*

—WINSTON CHURCHILL

When Jimmy Fallon was a college student, he worked as a humble intern at a newspaper in New York City. His boss connected Jimmy to entertainment agent Randi Siegel whose client roster included *Saturday Night Live* comedians David Spade and Adam Sandler. While Siegel admits she wasn't particularly blown away by Fallon's auditions, she was impressed by his knowledge of the comic industry and his attitude. Siegel helped Fallon on *SNL*, where Fallon invested a ton of time learning the logistics of how to put on a live television show.

Fallon loved the business and dedicated himself to learning everything he could. He focused on developing relationships. *SNL* producer Marci Klein liked Fallon and gave him some great advice early on: she told him to thank media giant and *SNL* founder Lorne Michaels after every show. Producer Michaels is famously busy and aloof. But week after week, Fallon thanked Michaels. After every single show. Eventually Michaels warmed to Fallon, and that relationship led Fallon to his first job hosting a late-night television show. Fallon's determination to overachieve in the small responsibilities kept leading to bigger opportunities. As host of his own late-night show, Jimmy Fallon made a point to reach out to Jay Leno, the producer and host of *The Tonight Show* at the time. Fallon sought Leno out for career advice and industry tips on how to handle the responsibilities of hosting his own show. These relationships—both with Michaels and Leno—ultimately led to Fallon taking over as host of *The Tonight Show* when Leno retired.

Jimmy Fallon's rise was a direct result of the time and intention he put into connecting with producers. He was always hungry to learn more about his craft and the entertainment industry. Many who know Fallon have commented that his meteoric rise has as much to do with his commitment to learn from producers of the entertainment world as it does his talent.[29]

WHO ARE THE PRODUCERS?

In Jimmy Fallon's story, producers are literally producing shows and movies. In Proximity Principle terms, producers are the men and women building businesses, running teams, and making decisions in your industry or field. They're the creators of jobs and opportunities. In publishing, they're publishers and acquisitions editors. In other areas, they're the directors of marketing, the vice presidents of sales, and the partners of CPA firms. They're also the superintendents of school districts and the general managers of sports franchises.

Their focus is always on the success of their own operation. This means that they aren't really concerned with your career journey, except as it pertains to the success of their own team. Their primary mission is to find the people who can help them win! Think of them as the gatekeepers to work that matters. Without their attention, there will be no opportunity. And your proximity to them will determine the opportunities you get to do meaningful and exciting work.

KEY QUALITIES OF PRODUCERS

Producers are high-achieving professionals, which usually means they are busy—really busy. They're always hard at work driving teams and projects to the finish line.

While producers have the power to quickly advance our journey, we can't expect to receive an immediate payoff (or on getting paid at all) when we connect with them. The payoff may take time, but it will be powerful. And keep in mind that you'll have to approach them differently than you do any of the other types of people we've talked about so far. That said, there are four key qualities producers provide that can help get you in closer proximity to your dream job:

1. They Share Knowledge
2. They Provide Connections
3. They Offer Opportunities
4. They Give Direction

Producers Share Knowledge

Access to producers helps us understand what we need to do to be successful. They're already building teams that win, so their judgment in evaluating competency and talent matters. Producers may offer constructive criticism and highlight what you still need to learn. Don't mistake producers for professors, though. They're not interested in helping you grow; they're interested in winning. Watch them and you'll learn what it takes to win.

Jeff, a caller on my show, decided to take an internship at a local studio editing music tracks as he pursued an audio engineering career. He was taking classes to learn the fundamentals during the day and practicing in the studio at night. Jeff began adding value to the recording studio by sharing new technology tips and techniques he was learning at school about newer, more updated software he was working with. The owner of the studio and the lead sound engineer gave Jeff more responsibility over time, as well as critical feedback on how he could improve. They weren't doing it for his benefit; they were doing it to win. And Jeff was okay with that! They were grateful for the help Jeff brought to their business, and Jeff was grateful for the knowledge he was gaining from being there.

Producers Provide Connections

In addition to sharing knowledge, producers can also help you make connections in your field. They inevitably know other producers, so approach every conversation with the understanding that they can connect you with someone who can help you on your climb. When you talk to a producer, don't act like you're on a job interview. While it's important to tell them where you want to go, your focus is to learn from them. These relationships can be incredibly beneficial to your career, even though it can be intimidating at first to seek out such high-achieving people. And remember that while they can truly help accelerate your climb, you have something to offer to them too!

Chris, a guy from Baltimore who called in one day, wanted to get into medical device design. After discovering his neighbor had a connection with the president of a local firm, Chris was given the opportunity to meet with him for fifteen minutes. Jay, the firm president, who didn't seem super excited about giving up fifteen minutes of his time, warned Chris that he had no available positions. But Chris pressed on. He told Jay he'd still like to meet to share his passion for the industry. They met, and a month later, Chris received a call from the CEO of a design firm in California. The CEO explained that he'd heard about Chris in a recent conversation at an industry conference with an acquaintance named Jay. Do you see what happened here? Chris gained an interview from the fifteen minutes he spent with a producer who wasn't even hiring! While it can often feel like taking the time to get to know producers doesn't give you immediate results, you never know how or when that one conversation with a producer will impact your future.

> YOU NEVER KNOW HOW OR WHEN THAT ONE CONVERSATION WITH A PRODUCER WILL IMPACT YOUR FUTURE.

Producers Offer Opportunities

Producers can also give you work opportunities that wouldn't otherwise be available to you. Now when I say "work opportunities," I don't necessarily mean paid jobs—although if you can get paid, that's great! Remember, producers are hiring, creating jobs, and putting together winning teams, and unpaid opportunities or internships allow you to grow your network with them. I can promise you that this work isn't wasted. Roger Goodell, the current commissioner of the National Football League, began his work as an NFL intern. Steven Spielberg, before he ever made a movie, interned with Universal Studios. And Clint Eastwood, Matt Damon, Ben Affleck, Brad Pitt, and Sylvester Stallone all began in minor roles or by accepting positions as extras on movie sets. The point here is: you need to value *any opportunity you can get from a producer.*

Producers Give Direction

Finally, producers can give you direction on where the marketplace is headed and what it will take to succeed there. Their insight is so valuable because they actually have access to the jobs and positions you want, and they can provide expert advice on the exact steps you should take to get there. They can share the ins and outs of an industry or discipline, helping you understand the expectations required of you. And producers can warn you of any pitfalls or obstacles that you might come up against so that you can better prepare yourself for the challenges ahead.

INTERACTING WITH PRODUCERS

When you first connect with a producer, one thing you absolutely don't want to do is ask for a job. Believe me. I made that mistake once. I was so fired up and enthusiastic about getting time with this producer that I actually asked if he would hire me. He didn't. And I'm also pretty sure he never met with me again. Instead, you should always approach producers with a posture of humility and a hunger to learn from them. Be prepared to ask good questions and respectfully make the most of your time with them. Articulate where you want to go in your career and listen closely to the advice and feedback they offer.

Trina called my show one day to ask for advice on how to change industries. She had all the qualifications to move into the tech industry, but she had no relationships or connections in this field. I suggested she find a producer who could tell her what it would take to cross over into that new industry. To her credit, she did her homework, talked to everyone she could, and found out there was a CEO of a local technology company who actually lived six houses down the street from her. So she connected with the neighbor and asked to take him to lunch. They had a fantastic lunch, and Trina took a moment to explain her desire to switch industries. She never once asked the guy for a job, but she did bring along a notepad and pen so that she could write down his guidance and advice.

The next day she sent a short, friendly follow-up email. It simply said, "Thank you for spending time with me. That was so encouraging." The CEO replied saying, "Absolutely. Let me know if you ever want to get together again." Several months later, the CEO emailed Trina again to tell her that his company had a position that he thought would be a good fit and asked her if she was interested!

Trina's story shows The Proximity Principle at work. She met a producer and didn't ask for a job. She sought advice, took notes on how to navigate her new career path, and left that lunch meeting equipped and encouraged. And I believe the producer walked away from that lunch impressed with Trina—with an antenna up about opportunities for her. As soon as something came across his desk, he thought of his neighbor. Now that's the power of having producers in your circle!

Help Them Win

Early in my career, I received some great input from a woman named Jen, who at the time was a director for Comcast Sports Southeast. My professor, Jeff, at the broadcasting school I attended in Atlanta, was able to get me a sit-down with her. I told her I had a concept that could be a show or at least a segment on the *Sports Night* program she produced. She liked my idea but clarified that she just didn't have the budget to hire me. At the end of the conversation, she let me know that if I was ever going to get the opportunity, I would need to put together a three-minute sample segment.

She explained exactly what I needed to do: create a segment using three cameras, clear audio, and great lighting—or the pitch would not stand a chance. These were things I hadn't learned yet, so I took notes on everything she said, along with the specific instructions, and then reached out to a guy named Rob Mottola. Rob was a director and producer I met through mutual friends, and I knew if anyone could help me pull this off, it would be him. He offered to come over and shoot the segment, and he even edited it for me. Once it was finished, I delivered the segment to Jen, and fortunately she liked it enough to put it on the air. Then she invited me to follow it up with four or five more segments. I did all of this for free and paid for it out of my own pocket, but I was able to prove to myself that I could get something on television. This project was probably one of the biggest momentum shifts in my career. I realized through that experience that if you help people win, they will open a door of opportunity for you.

> IF YOU HELP PEOPLE WIN, THEY WILL OPEN A DOOR OF OPPORTUNITY FOR YOU.

Because of their positions and experience, producers have the power to advise you, hire you, and connect you to others in ways that could speed you along on the path to your dream job. They can choose you for their team or recommend you to others looking for just the right person. The attitude and effort you bring to your interactions with them can make all the difference. In fact, I would go as far as to say your career advancement depends on your proximity to them. So make it a priority to invest some of your time with them. You won't regret it!

THE PROXIMITY PROCESS

1. Make a list of companies and organizations in your desired field, then find out who the producers are.

2. Determine exactly what you want to learn about their industry, then write down a few key questions you'd like to ask them.

3. Schedule a brief meeting (in person or by phone) to learn about their industry.

PART 2

THE PLACES

Success doesn't come to you. You go to it.

—MARVA COLLINS

Climbing a mountain must be done in stages. No climber, no matter how skilled, should rush a climb. The reality is, every climb begins with a trek into the foothills of the mountain. Then, there are acclimation climbs where you stop to rest, allowing your body to adjust to the strains of elevation. Next, there's a short expedition to the basecamp where you organize your gear, check the weather, and prepare for the actual climb. Finally, if everything up to this point checks out, you can begin your approach to the summit—the last leg of the climb, requiring the most advanced climbing techniques.

As you begin your climb, think of these stages as the *places* that will get you in proximity to your dream job. Each place prepares you for the next. In mountain-climbing terms, climbers can't charge up a mountain at a reckless pace without going through each stage. There are no shortcuts to the summit.

EVERY PLACE MATTERS

Believe me, I would have loved to take a few shortcuts as I climbed my personal Mount Everest. But spending time in each stage is just part of the deal. If I had skipped any of the places on my climb (broadcasting school, my internship at the sports radio station, launching my first podcast, and the Saturday afternoon radio show), I would have missed the opportunity to learn, practice, perform, and grow. What I learned from my successes—and my many failures—equipped me for my dream job. As leadership expert John Maxwell puts it, "Growth is the great separator between those who succeed and those who do not." Growth takes time. It's not something you can be impatient with. And don't let limiting beliefs (fear and pride) convince you that these stages are unnecessary or that there's some way to avoid the work required to accomplish your climb. On your Proximity Principle climb, each place will prepare you for long-term success.

Let's look at journalist and TV host Katie Couric's career. Couric was regarded as one of the most successful—and popular—newscasters in America until she stepped out of news broadcasting. But there were no shortcuts for Couric on her climb. In fact, right out of college her very first job was as a desk assistant at ABC. It took her nearly thirty years of work-ing hard in place after place before she became the first-ever solo female evening news anchor at CBS.[30] Early in her career, Couric knew that getting in proximity to the right people in the right places was important as long as you use each place to grow. During an interview several

> ON YOUR PROXIMITY PRINCIPLE CLIMB, EACH PLACE WILL PREPARE YOU FOR LONG-TERM SUCCESS.

years ago, Couric said, "I have been at the right place at the right time. If I didn't have the work ethic to back it up, it would have been a short-lived thing."[31] Couric understood that each step of your climb requires time and effort. The lessons and growth you gain from each place are essential and will play a huge role in bringing you more opportunities.

The Five Places

As you get in proximity to your dream job, there are five places you can expect to encounter on your climb:

1. **The place where you are.** Everything you need to get started is right in your very own zip code.
2. **A place to learn.** This is where you'll obtain the education, certifications, and knowledge you need to be successful.
3. **A place to practice.** Education becomes experience at this stage.
4. **A place to perform.** Moving from practice to performance happens here.
5. **A place to grow.** This is the inner ring of proximity—within striking distance of your dream.

Now let's take a closer look at these so you know how to carry them out in The Proximity Principle!

CHAPTER 7

THE PLACE WHERE YOU ARE

Start where you are. Do what you can. Use what you have.

—ARTHUR ASHE

People often call into my radio show to ask me where they need to go to begin their climb toward work that matters. Some folks think they need to pick up and move to a new city before they even get started, and that's simply not true. The truth is, when you are getting started, you're rarely limited by your location. No matter where you live, you can get in closer proximity to your dream job.

TURN OVER EVERY ROCK

Starting where you are requires something I like to call "turning over rocks." You may have heard the phrase "leave no stone unturned." That just means you are going to do everything you can think of to find or get something. Well "turning over rocks" is my way of communicating a work ethic that leads to success, and all it means is that you look for opportunities in unlikely places.

> THE TRUTH IS, YOU ARE RARELY LIMITED BY YOUR LOCATION.

I knew that talking in front of people was part of what I wanted to do, but I needed to do a little research and discovery to see what that could look like as a career. In this discovery phase, I felt like I needed to get in some speaking gigs to build up my resumé, so I went out looking for *any* place I could find that would allow me to emcee live events. One of the first jobs I found was introducing clowns. Yep, that's right. Clowns. I had heard that the summer festival in my town, Suwanee, Georgia, needed an emcee, so I reached out and was chosen for the job. Now let's be real here. Very few people were actually jumping at this opportunity. So there I was, on one of the hottest days of summer, sweating in the Georgia heat, to introduce clowns, jugglers, local musicians, and even guys who made balloon animals! If ever there was an opportunity to practice humility and set my pride aside, this was it! But I knew I had to do anything and everything to get better—even if that meant pretending to be excited about balloon animals. Keeping these crowds engaged wasn't exactly easy. I don't think a single person was actually listening to the words coming out of my mouth, yet this was still practice for me. It affirmed that I really love the energy and excitement of speaking on a stage, and it allowed me to add another bullet of experience to my resumé.

> SEIZING OPPORTUNITIES WHEREVER YOU CAN FIND THEM WILL ALLOW YOU TO LEARN MORE ABOUT YOURSELF IN RELATION TO YOUR DREAM JOB.

No one was knocking on my door to ask me to emcee events. I knew that *if it was going to be, it was up to me.* I chased down every opportunity and volunteered. I turned over every rock I could to find small, local events that would let me get on stage. The pay was never much, but it was exciting work, and each emcee opportunity allowed me to do what I really enjoyed—connect with a live audience from the stage. Even though I wasn't doing exactly what I wanted to do, I was experiencing proximity to my dream job, using the talents and skills I'd need someday. Turning over rocks will condition you to look for opportunities wherever you can find them. And seizing those opportunities—any opportunity—will allow you to learn more about yourself in relation to your dream job. This discovery phase is such an important part of the process. Don't miss it!

My friend Brad was passionate and driven to get into the film business. The problem was, he and his family were settled in Charlotte, North Carolina, and the thought of moving at that time was overwhelming. Still, Brad believed that all the film work was done in Hollywood. In his mind there were so many hurdles to clear to pursue his dream. He needed to sell his house. His wife would need to find a new job. The kids would have to change schools. From his perspective, all these things needed to happen or he wouldn't make any progress. I challenged Brad to research the Charlotte area to see how many production studios were based there. With a little research, Brad found out there were well over one hundred!

So Brad decided to begin where he was, turning over rocks in Charlotte. It wasn't long before he landed a job as a production assistant at a studio just blocks away from his home. And even though he knew he wanted to work in film, he wasn't sure about the specifics of this kind of job. In his role as a production assistant, Brad learned more about the nuances of the field, and it confirmed that he loved the idea of being a video producer. He didn't have to change zip codes to start working toward his goal. Fast forward several years. Brad has now reached his summit and is working in Hollywood. He did eventually move his family across the country, but he was able to learn more about the industry and earn valuable experience without ever changing his address. The point here is that you don't have to pack up and change locations to start climbing. You just have to use what I call "The Law of the Zip Code."

THE LAW OF THE ZIP CODE

The Law of the Zip Code is simple and liberating. It states: everything you need to get started is within your reach. You don't need to move across the country or even rent office space. You can simply start with what you have. Many of the most successful business people did this very thing by starting out not just in their own zip codes but in their *garages*! Walt Disney, creator of one of the highest-grossing media companies on the planet launched his company in his uncle's cramped one-car garage. Walt didn't need the perfect location to start some of his earlier animations. He simply used some creativity and what he had available—some spare lumber and old boxes for an animation stand and a tiny garage for a studio—and got to work.[32]

And many other companies did this same thing. Jeff Bezos's launched a little company called Amazon in his garage. Steve Jobs started Apple in a garage. And one of the world's biggest producers of business equipment,

93

Hewlett-Packard, began in a garage. Location had no bearing on the success of their work, and it shouldn't for you either. So don't believe that you've got to go looking for space to rent to start a new thing. Just move that old Camry or Chevy out of the garage and into the driveway and get started. If Amazon and Apple began this way, you can too.

The Basics of Starting in Your Zip Code

The truth about The Proximity Principle is that if you have enough grit, you can always find an opportunity to get started right where you are. Of course there are some basics you need to keep in mind about this early stage of the journey. First, start looking for jobs in the broader industry of what you want to do. Second, go after something that's interesting to you and somehow related to the work you want to do long term. And third, remember that this is just the beginning stage. Anything worth doing is going to take patience and time.

> IF YOU HAVE ENOUGH GRIT, YOU CAN ALWAYS FIND AN OPPORTUNITY TO GET STARTED RIGHT WHERE YOU ARE.

During one episode of *The Ken Coleman Show*, I had the chance to interview two cousins living in Los Angeles. Jim Tselikis and Sabin Lomac, founders of Cousins Maine Lobster, personify the principle of beginning where you are. Their story began in 2011 while playing games one night on an old Nintendo console. The cousins began reminiscing about growing up in Maine, and eventually started talking about food. They got excited remembering what it was like to eat delicious Maine lobster on a regular basis. And then an idea hit. They wondered what it would take to start a lobster food truck business to give people on the West Coast the experience of a Maine lobster shack. So they set out to make it happen.

In April of 2012, they celebrated opening day with their first truck right there in Los Angeles, a town not exactly known for great lobster. Of course they never dreamed of the success that first day would bring. News spread via social media and word of mouth, and within days, they were offered a spot on the reality TV show *Shark Tank*, followed by an investment deal with Barbara Corcoran from the show. Now they have dozens of food trucks in nineteen cities and several brick-and-mortar restaurants too! From the start, their business was met with rave reviews, and now the real-life cousins who brought in $20 million last year alone are sharing the food from their childhood with people across the country—including my hometown of Nashville. And the best part? It all started in their own zip code.[33]

These cousins could have limited themselves because of where they lived. They could have thought that moving back to Maine was the only way to make their dream happen. But they didn't believe that moving was a necessity. And you shouldn't either. When it comes to The Proximity Principle, your physical location should never be considered an obstacle. You absolutely do not have to change zip codes to get started! You just have to start.

THE LONG VIEW

As you begin where you are, it will help if you embrace a long view of the climb. If you don't, you'll become impatient and you may choose to give up. Remember, this is just the beginning. There are going to be many stages along the way, and all of them are going to offer you opportunities to learn and grow. You must accept—and expect—that it's going to take a while, and there will be roadblocks and detours to navigate.

Kara called into my show one day to talk about her passion for animation. She had her Mount Everest in mind—to one day work for Pixar Studios. She was twenty-one years old and just starting out, but she understood she needed experience animating. So Kara began contacting local businesses in her area that worked in television advertising and volunteered to do animation for them. For the next few years, Kara focused on three things: eating, sleeping, and animating. And the more she animated, the more she added to her animation portfolio. All of her hard work led to a paid internship with a local television station—an opportunity she was really excited about. But that opportunity came only after Kara focused for three years on building her skill set. Kara has a long way to go to get to her dream job, but she is determined to become the very best animator she can be. And I'm certain she is well on her way.

Just like Kara, you must keep the long view in mind. It may take three years before a door opens for you, but don't give up. By starting where you are and putting in the hard work necessary, opportunity will come.

THE PROXIMITY PROCESS

1. Turn over every rock in your zip code and surrounding areas. Make a list of every place that is doing something in your desired field.

2. Determine what jobs or volunteer opportunities are available at those companies that you could do.

3. Talk to your family, friends, and acquaintances to find out if they know someone that works in those companies to get connected to that opportunity.

CHAPTER 8

A PLACE TO LEARN

*The more that you learn, the
more places you'll go.*

—DR. SEUSS

Ashley is passionate about health and fitness. For several years she'd been at home full time with her kids, and once her kids were all in school, she was feeling anxious about reentering the work force. She dreamed of being a fitness trainer, but her college degree was in accounting. An office job held zero appeal. She was seriously considering going back to college to earn a different degree, but she wasn't sure it would be worth the time and money. Then one day when she was working out at her local gym, she saw a sign that read "Childcare Worker Needed." The position itself wasn't her dream job, but it was something she felt completely qualified to do, and it was a good first step to get her in proximity to what she really wanted to do. She'd found the right place to learn.

Ashley got the job and quickly found her values and temperament were a good match for the company's culture. Her supervisor at the gym took notice and offered Ashley on-the-job training—classes in nutrition, CPR, weight training, physiology, and ultimately certification for personal training. She did all of this training while still working hard at her childcare position, and the more training she completed, the more it fueled her passion. And now? Ashley has transitioned to working as a certified personal trainer, and she's loving it!

DETERMINE YOUR NEXT STEP

Doing some research and training on the front end will do one of two things for you: it will either affirm your passion or steer you in another direction altogether. None of your research will be wasted if it helps you determine next steps. That was exactly the case with a guy named Cameron who called into my show. Cameron called to talk about his dream of being a surgical neurologist. Now that's a big dream! Hearing him talk made me feel a little unqualified to be giving this guy advice! I knew he was serious about becoming a surgeon when he told me that he'd spent several hours watching brain surgery videos online. Can you imagine watching several hours of brain surgery footage? Folks, if this isn't evidence of passion, I don't know what is. Cameron's research confirmed that medical school was the next right place for him to learn, and now that's exactly where he is.

To School or Not to School?

Your passion to learn will drive you and help you discover your next best step. The research itself can give you a great deal of insight, showing you the knowledge and skills you'll need to do what you want to do. Then once you understand *what* you need to learn, you can turn your attention to researching *where* you need to learn it. Spend some time on these questions:

1. What schools offer that degree or what trade school offers that certification?
2. Who's teaching the craft?
3. What's the best training program out there?
4. Is the program affordable?
5. Does it fit in your current budget?

Ultimately you want to find a place that specializes and is recognized for training people to do what you want to do.

This can often feel a little overwhelming. It raises a lot of questions for people, as they aren't sure what that transition should look like from getting where they are now to where they want to be. People who want to move into a new job often ask, "Should I quit my job and go back to school?" I get this question on my radio show a lot. My answer? Not necessarily.

YOUR PASSION TO LEARN WILL DRIVE YOU AND HELP YOU DISCOVER YOUR NEXT BEST STEP.

Every job requires skills and knowledge, but not every job requires a degree or certification. If you're not sure what kind of education your dream job requires, talk to the producers and professionals in your field. They will know what qualifications and experience you'll truly need and will be able to show you the different paths to get to your destination.

A Different Kind of School

If you want it badly enough, you can find the right place to learn no matter where you are. I came across a story recently of someone who perfectly illustrates this concept. This guy grew up a movie fan. Now I know a lot of folks say they love movies, but this person loved them so much that his personal Mount Everest was to become a filmmaker. In fact, he was so sure he wanted to make movies that he found a job in a local video store where he worked for the next several years making just a few bucks an hour. He wasn't just passing the time. He used the place he was in as an opportunity to learn by watching literally hundreds, if not thousands, of movies. He intently studied the films for their dialogue, plot twists, shots, camera angles, and lighting. And he took mental notes on techniques that would eventually add to his own style.

Who was this guy? None other than the award-winning, Quentin Tarantino. Those years spent watching movies in a video store didn't earn him a certificate or a diploma. In fact, you probably would have looked at that kid and thought he was wasting his life away, hanging out in a video store, watching movies, and working for nearly nothing. But Tarantino used that place as a school. All those notes he took were filed away for future reference. He committed the scenes and plot twists from all the Kung Fu films, crime capers, and horror flicks he watched to memory and used elements of them in his later work. That little video store gave him some of the best education and learnings he needed to become one of the most famous filmmakers of our time.[34]

> EVERY JOB REQUIRES SKILLS AND KNOWLEDGE, BUT NOT EVERY JOB REQUIRES A DEGREE OR CERTIFICATION.

If you're committed, you'll find a way to get the education you need to get into proximity to work that matters.

I'm sure there are plenty of filmmakers who'd love to have some of the opportunities and successes that Tarantino has achieved professionally, but how many of them would actually be willing to spend years making minimum wage to get there? Finding your own place to learn will take time and energy, and when you do find it, it will take patience and persistence to gather the knowledge you need. But—just like Tarantino—you aren't limited by where you can start your learning!

Traditional vs. Nontraditional Education

You may discover that the path to your dream career does require traditional education. My friend Matthew was a successful executive for an international import firm. In the course of his work there, Matthew discovered a passion for negotiating contracts, so he decided to find out what it would take to move into one of those positions. He learned he needed to earn an advanced degree in international trade law, so that is what he did. And he did it with his company's encouragement and an education benefit to help pay for it! He's now doing exactly what he wants to do and was able to get a quality education to do it.

Traditional colleges require students to take basic general education courses called "101s" before you move on to the major-specific courses that train you in your field. Don't assume that your 101 courses can only be found in traditional academic settings. It's also possible to get your 101s in by observing professionals in the workplace or spending time in proximity to the product you'll be producing. For example, Wes had a passion for art and dreamed of becoming a skilled artist. He took a part-time job as a security guard at a renowned art museum, which gave him time to observe the master works of painters he admired and to listen in on conversations of people interacting with the art. At home, Wes spent countless hours in his studio drawing, painting, and studying the great artists whose works appeared at the museum. Those hours he spent learning at the museum were a huge investment in his education, and it did not cost him a dime. He was being paid while he learned.

Universities, community colleges, and trade schools are great places to learn, but they're not for everyone. Sure, you must be knowledgeable and educated in your craft, but knowledge can be found both inside and outside of a classroom. You may find that the traditional academic setting isn't the direction you need to go to get in proximity to your dream job. When I decided to attend Jeff Batten's broadcasting school in Atlanta, I knew that I didn't need a degree. What I needed was a place to learn the fundamentals before I went out to practice in a work environment. That nontraditional educational setting equipped me with many of the basic skills I still use in my broadcasting work today.

Another option to consider is online education or trade-specific schools. Depending on the type of work you're pursuing it's possible to find the professors you need in certification programs or trade schools—and they may even be a better fit for you. Bart, for example, was working in construction when he decided he wanted to specialize as an electrician and open his own business. So he found a trade school to learn that craft, and before he even finished the program, he had multiple job offers. He's now a happy and successful business owner.

Keep Your Day Job

The thought of going back to school or investing time in learning a new job can be intimidating, especially if you've got bills to pay. Not everyone can just quit working for as long as it takes to learn a whole new gig. But here's some good news: you can keep your existing job while pursuing your education on the side. Justin, a guy I met, did just that. He wanted to teach art to young people, so he enrolled in a master's program that met on the weekends at a local university. That flexible schooling option gave him the knowledge he needed to land a job at an art school without interfering with his day job in the process.

And my friend Ann was able to do the same thing. While working at a hospital, she realized her passion for helping people and decided to become an RN. She found a great nursing program at a local community college and continued working at the hospital while she attended classes on nights and weekends. And she did that until she finished her degree! Those are just two examples of people who didn't just quit their jobs cold turkey. They were able to find educational options that worked with their busy work schedules, so they could continue bringing in an income and providing for themselves and their families.

Also consider taking online classes, reading books, and participating in webinars. You can get great training these days through online programs or even just reading a book, so don't limit yourself to thinking that it has to happen in a formal classroom.

THE CULTURE OF A PROFESSION

Finding a place you can learn will give you access to the culture of a profession. What do I mean by that? The culture of a profession is simply all the things that make up a workplace: the people, the mission of the place, employees' attitudes and the way they work together, the company morale, even down to the feel of the place when you walk in. Gaining access to a company's culture can help you clearly understand how what you want to do fits into the industry as a whole. As you learn about a role you are interested in, this will either confirm your direction or push you to change direction to a role you are better suited for.

My friend Zoe knew she wanted to work in the A&R (artists and repertoire) department at a record company. It's what she'd studied for in school. She made phone calls and knocked on doors until she found an internship on Music Row in Nashville. In her time there, she picked up on the culture of the company: how people dressed, how they talked, how they divided responsibilities. In fact, she discovered that the role of an A&R person was different at a small record label than from what she'd learned in her college classes. Zoe's place to learn equipped her to understand the culture of the industry enough to land her first job!

And in some ways, my first broadcasting internship at the local sports talk radio station in Atlanta taught me similar things. I poured coffee for the radio hosts and looked up things on YouTube for them while they did their show. I didn't play a huge role, I never sat behind a microphone, and I didn't get paid a dime, but I was able to observe, learn, and get a much-needed perspective. I went from being a complete outsider to knowing the lingo and the culture. This is what a place to learn can offer you on your climb, and that's why this stage is so important.

A CHANCE TO SEE THE FUTURE

It can be intimidating to jump into learning something new at first, but don't allow yourself to stay stuck in work that doesn't matter to you and that you have no passion for. You can do this! See places of learning as an opportunity to look into the future and imagine yourself working in that role. Set aside those limiting beliefs of pride and fear, and take on the challenge of pushing yourself closer to your dream job. The knowledge you gain will help you decide for sure if this is the career you want to go after. It's why aspiring teachers sit in on classroom teaching to observe seasoned teachers at work. It's why medical students often shadow an experienced ER doctor. They're all asking: Is this where I want to be? Is this what I want to do with my life?

SEE PLACES OF LEARNING AS AN OPPORTUNITY TO LOOK INTO THE FUTURE AND IMAGINE YOURSELF WORKING IN THAT ROLE.

Your time observing and learning will give you a strong sense of the work you're aiming for, motivating you to keep moving toward your dream job. It will help you find clarity about the things you enjoy. And you'll gain the knowledge you need to move to the next vital stage of your journey—finding a place to practice!

THE PROXIMITY PROCESS

1. Make a list of places that are recognized for training people in what you need to learn.

2. Determine how much it will cost.

3. Decide how much you can afford, then calculate how long it will take to complete the education based on the availability of your time and money.

CHAPTER 9

A PLACE TO PRACTICE

*I think we all learn by doing rather
than thinking about doing.*

—JENNIFER WESTFELDT

In your place to practice, you'll start to convert education into execution! No matter what field you're pursuing, a place to practice is essential. It allows you to get in
the reps you need to improve and prepares you for a real
role doing what you want to do.

Doctors are a good example of this. They spend years
training in their field. After going through eight years of
formal education—four years for an undergraduate degree
plus another four years (at least) for medical school—they

then spend an additional three to seven years in a residency program. That's their place to practice. It's real experience with real patients. Aren't you thankful medical students aren't thrown into life-or-death situations right away? I know I am.

Years ago I broke my thumb, tearing the ligament in two. When the doctor told me I needed surgery to regain the use of it, I never questioned whether or not he was going to do a good job. I trusted that based on his credentials (of finishing medical school), his practice (during residency), and his further practice and experience (on the job), he would repair my thumb like new. No one would go into surgery confidently if they were the first patient that surgeon had ever operated on! That just doesn't happen. Medical students practice for hours and hours before they ever get to step foot in an operating room to perform surgery. And you'll need to do the same as you pursue your dream job.

WHAT YOU STAND TO GAIN

When you spend time practicing what you have learned and observed from the experts in your industry—the professionals and the producers who are experiencing a ton of success—you'll quickly discover the payoff of practicing your craft. Here's what you'll gain from the hours of practice you put in:

1. Real Experience
2. Feedback
3. Freedom to Fail
4. Wins

Arnold Palmer is someone who gained everything from the many hours and years he spent practicing golf. His father gave him his first set of golf clubs when he was only three years old, and as a young boy, Palmer played golf every chance he got. At age eleven, Palmer started working as a caddie and was spending even more time practicing and analyzing golf courses. He was awarded a golf scholarship to Wake Forest College in North Carolina but dropped out after one of his best friends was killed in a car accident. He spent some time in the service, even building a nine-hole course to practice on at his training center. Then once his enlistment term ended, he decided to participate in the U.S. Amateur golf tournament in 1954. And he won. Four years later Palmer won the Masters Tournament.[35] That victory and the numerous other victories and awards Palmer earned were the result of hours upon hours and years upon years of practice. Palmer joked about the amount of time he practiced: "It's a funny thing," he said. "The more I practice, the luckier I get." And while he did seem to have a stroke of good luck—with multiple wins and being the first person ever to make a million dollars in earnings playing golf—his success had much more to do with the amount of time he spent practicing.[36]

You Gain Real Experience

Malcolm Gladwell popularized the importance of practice in his book *Outliers* when he introduced what he calls the 10,000-hour rule. The rule simply states that it takes 10,000 hours of practice to become an expert at anything. While that theory has come under some scrutiny in the last few years, the examples Gladwell uses in his book are pretty compelling. One of those is his story of The Beatles and how playing club shows helped them become one of the best rock bands in history.

In the summer of 1960, The Beatles packed up and moved from their home in England to Hamburg, Germany. The first nightclub they signed to play in expected them to perform Monday through Friday for four and a half hours each night, and then on the weekends for six hours a night. And they did this for forty-eight nights straight! Talk about gaining some experience! Over the next two years, the band kept this exhausting schedule at various venues around the city, perfecting their craft, their sound, their style, and, of course, their famous haircuts. Those little nightclubs in Germany were more than just a place to practice; they were the start of an incredible climb that led to music sales of more than 178 million albums.[37]

The Average Joe

Now listen, I know what you're probably thinking. Not everyone wants to be in a rock band, and certainly not everyone can drop everything to get experience in a place to practice like The Beatles did. I get it. But getting real experience doesn't have to be that complicated. Let's look at Jordan.

Jordan loved coffee, but it wasn't her passion. Her passion was working with children. She dreamed of a teaching career, and she was working nights as a barista to pay for her early childhood education degree at the local community college. Jordan enjoyed working with kids so much that she volunteered with her church's children's ministry, devoting several hours each weekend to serving children and their families. She loved what she was doing, and it showed. One of the families at her church noticed how good she was with the kids and asked her to be their personal nanny. Not only was Jordan able to get more real-life experience with school-aged kids, but it was a paid gig with free room and board! Jordan was able to quit the barista job and focus on practicing the skills and techniques she was learning in her early childhood education classes. Now she could truly pursue her passion—and enjoy her barista coffee again without having to make it herself!

> GETTING REAL EXPERIENCE DOESN'T HAVE TO BE COMPLICATED.

Or consider Frank. He worked in corporate finance where he discovered a passion for building and real estate. He didn't want to leave his job, and he knew he had a lot to learn before jumping in full time. So he started small, planning and executing changes to his own home, eventually selling it for a profit. He ripped up and refinished floors, replaced drywall, tore out walls, remodeled the kitchen and baths, and bought more paint than he ever thought possible. Then after flipping almost a dozen personal residences where he could practice his skills and learn from his mistakes, he stepped out into building for others. Now he's left his corporate job and has his own commercial building company.

You Gain Feedback

Let's go back to Jordan, the barista-turned-nanny, for a minute. As Jordan continued her formal training to become a teacher, one of the requirements was to complete hours of student teaching. Student teachers spend time with a professional in the classroom where they can put theory into real practice to see if what they've read in textbooks works with actual students. As they get classroom experience, a professional teacher is there to guide them and give feedback. With an experienced teacher in the room to act as a safety net, student teachers can practice, fail, and try again. Most teachers would tell you that their time spent student teaching was invaluable. It gives them real-time feedback that they are then able to use in their own classrooms.

Professional athletes understand the value of feedback too. Practice time on the field isn't just a place for conditioning, to do reps, or to grow as a team. It's an opportunity to get feedback from their coaches and the other players. Relying on feedback to practice and improve isn't just for rookies. It's a way of life for seasoned athletes like Tom Brady,[38] Kobe Bryant,[39] and Serena Williams.[40] They dedicate hours to studying game films to get both visual feedback and to hear their coach's perspective on what went right or wrong. Then they apply that feedback to their practice time and scrimmages, trying out new techniques on the court or field, and conditioning and strengthening their bodies with workouts. But even the greatest athletes test out what they've learned in practice and in scrimmages. Why? Those are the places where they're free to experiment, innovate, and make mistakes.

> RELYING ON FEEDBACK TO PRACTICE AND IMPROVE ISN'T JUST FOR ROOKIES.

Getting feedback on your work can be intimidating, especially when you're stepping into something you're so passionate about. But your place to practice doesn't have to feel like a high-pressure situation. Many practice spaces aren't even physical locations. Practice in a "virtual" space can be low-pressure—and convenient. I recently met Rachel, an editor who wants to be a published author. The distance between editor and author doesn't seem that far, but even though she's been editing professionally for years, Rachel didn't feel confident submitting her work to publishers without some real writing experience. She really needed some feedback before she felt comfortable calling herself a writer. I suggested she begin posting some of her creative writing regularly on free online platforms. That way she can have her work read and critiqued in a non-threatening environment. Plus, she'd get used to writing goals and deadlines. Feedback from online readers seemed like a low-pressure idea, so she posted some of her writing, got some helpful suggestions from online readers, and continues to crank out content and look for opportunities to write.

You Gain the Freedom to Fail

Like Rachel, you're probably passionate about your dream job. And the thought of losing that passion because of failure may scare the heck out of you. You might even prefer never to try rather than risk failure. But remember, you've got to call this for what it is: pride and fear. These are lies that threaten to keep you from moving closer to your dream job. Like I said earlier: success often happens not *despite* failure but *because* of failure. Failing is an essential part of practice. Naturally nobody *wants* to fail, but if you view your place to practice as an opportunity to safely fail, taking those risks will be easier.

Jeff Bezos has made a name for himself not just as the CEO of Amazon, but for encouraging a culture of failure there. It's not that Bezos likes to fail. He doesn't. In fact, he even compares failure to having a root canal without anesthesia. That's nobody's idea of a good time. Regardless,

Bezos celebrates failures at Amazon because it means things are happening. People are inventing. Creating. Trying. He understands that creativity and innovation are critical to success, and failure is a critical part of creativity and innovation.[41] "If you only do things where you know the answer in advance, your company goes away," Bezos says.[42]

If you really want to reach the top of the mountain, you've got to adopt Bezos's philosophy on failure: to succeed you must try out new things and mess up. And as you look for places to practice, try to find places that understand failure is an essential part of the process. This can actually speed up your development. My friend Brady told me a great story about his first year interning at the accounting firm where he's now a partner. He made a terrible mistake on a receivables spreadsheet that could've cost his firm thousands of dollars. But the firm had controls in place for interns. His boss caught his mistake and taught him how to correct it. It wasn't the last mistake he'd make, but he was able to learn a valuable lesson without it impacting the company—and all under the safety net of the company. So as hard as it is, you've got to walk forward even into uncertainty. You won't have all the answers and you will fall down, but you'll learn from your mistakes and become better because of them.

Practicing without Pressure

Along with practicing in a place that encourages failure, it's helpful to practice in a place with little pressure, in a place where the stakes aren't so high. Kevin Hagewood—his clients call him "Kelvis"—is co-owner of an elite men's barbershop called Nashville Beard and Barber. Kevin has won awards for his beard styling. This creative barber spent years mastering his techniques. He first went to barber school where certification requires practice on mannequins or live models before the students ever give their first haircut to an actual client. Imagine being the one sitting in the barber's chair as a guinea pig for someone who had never practiced the art of a straight razor shave. No thank you! I'd rather my barber know exactly how to handle a razor—and to have plenty of practice on people other than me first. I'm guessing most people would agree, and that's why practicing on mannequins allows barbers to develop their skills in a place where there's very little risk and pressure. There's no doubt this gave Hagewood some of the creative freedom he needed to become a master barber and an award-winning beard stylist. This type of environment—where the pressure isn't so heavy it paralyzes you—can be both freeing and empowering. It will help you refine your craft so that you can win!

You Gain Wins

As important as it is to be in a place where you're free to fail, you also want to find a place where you can get some wins. These wins will give you the confidence you need to keep climbing your mountain and will give you opportunities that you haven't had before.

My friend Amy is a great example of this. Amy loved interior decorating and wanted to launch a company staging homes for real estate agents. Because she had no real marketable experience, she created her own place to practice by calling real estate agents and offering to stage their houses for free. "Free" held serious appeal for these folks, so they took a chance on Amy. The risk level was relatively low, and there was certainly room to fail, but Amy was passionate, knowledgeable, and professional in her approach. It was a safe and easy way to get real experience and gain some wins. Amy did such an unbelievable job with those first stagings that the real estate agents called her back—again and again, and now she runs one of the most sought-after staging companies in town!

> WHEN YOU'RE TURNING OVER ROCKS, LOOK FOR PLACES WHERE YOUR SUCCESS ADDS VALUE TO THE ENTIRE TEAM OR COMPANY.

Personal wins like Amy's are the fun part of practicing your craft. But it's even more rewarding when you can help your peers win in their place to practice too. It also shows that you aren't only in it for yourself and that you are a team player. So when you're turning over rocks, look for places where your success adds value to the entire team or company. James did this and called my show to share his success story with me. He made the practice squad of an NFL franchise as a defensive lineman in his first year out of college. James was part of the scout team—a team whose sole purpose is to prepare the starters for the next game by learning and imitating the upcoming opponent's offense and defense. In this role, James was able to improve his techniques, and with each practice, he got stronger and better. As a result, he was able to seriously challenge the starting offensive linemen who had to practice against him each week. Because of James's hard work, he was able to grow in his own skills and knowledge of the game and help the starters get more prepared for their big games on Sunday.

Both Amy and James put themselves in places where they could not only get practice in, but also achieve personal wins while adding value to the peers and professionals around them. That's the best kind of win-win—when people get to experience the success of their own win while helping others achieve their own.

FINDING A PLACE TO PRACTICE

Finding a place to practice takes dedication and grit, but don't be afraid to start small. Remember, every stage prepares you for the next. It will take some sacrifice, but every worthy endeavor does, especially on the climb to your dream job.

My Place to Practice

As I was looking for places to practice, some of the opportunities I found really tested my resolve. One of those was working as an announcer for high school football games in Georgia. I took this gig while I was attending the eight-week class in Jeff's broadcasting school, so my time was already at a minimum. And it was an hour away from my house! But the chance to get in front of a mic was compelling enough for me to make the sacrifice.

I had an interesting mix of emotions on that long drive to the school. Obviously I was excited about the opportunity. I'd been practicing this type of play-by-play announcing in class, and this was my chance to actually do it and see what I was made of. I was also nervous and embarrassed. I mean, what would people think of a guy in his thirties spending his Friday nights in a tiny booth doing play-by-play for a high school football game? Some nights as I was driving to the games, I actually thought about turning around. But I didn't.

And when the pre-game broadcast started, it was game on—literally! At first whistle, I came alive. My fears subsided because I had done my preparation. Now I'll admit my announcing was not stellar, but my effort sure was. My entire attitude shifted as I focused on practicing what I'd been learning. And I loved sports, so this was fun for me! The game flew by and I was a bit disappointed when the final buzzer sounded. Overall I did pretty well, made no major mistakes, and felt pretty confident that I could get a lot better.

Offering Your Services

On your climb, you may have to knock on doors and offer your services to a number of people in order to find a place to practice. You may find a gig that's an hour away. And you may have to offer your services for free. But if you truly want to practice, you are going to have to go out and ask ten people in order to find four who will give you an opportunity!

My friend Jennifer got her foot in the door by offering her services for free. Jennifer wanted to be a floral designer for weddings and large events. To get some practice she offered to do flower arrangements for free at several weddings as long as the client paid for the cost of the actual flowers. As a single mom, putting in extra time that she wasn't getting paid for was tough, but it was exactly the right place for her to practice coordinating flower arrangements on a larger scale. That practice gave her the experience she needed to open a small business offering floral design services in her home state. And she's also the preferred vendor for some of the nicest resorts in the south. Not a bad payoff for a few free wedding gigs!

Brian is another friend who volunteered his time for an opportunity. Brian wanted to cross over from book marketing to marketing music, so he began volunteering to help with events at a local record label for free every evening after working his day job. It was a demanding and difficult phase of his climb. Volunteering every evening meant he had to say no to nearly everything else in his life. But he knew this phase was temporary and it would give him an opportunity to learn from and connect with people in the music industry. And now, just a few years later, he's the vice president of marketing at a prominent record label.

It Doesn't Have to Be Complicated

Finding a place to practice doesn't have to be complicated. If you want to pursue a career in digital marketing, help a friend set up his or her website. Want to become a mechanic? Start by working on your own car. If you want to speak publicly, consider joining Toastmasters and find opportunities to speak at schools, nonprofits, and business clubs. If you'd like to open your own nursery selling plants, try working a shift on the weekend at your local garden center in addition to your day job. And if your dream is to work at a recording studio, take a gig helping set up equipment at a local music venue a night a week. No matter what you want to do, find a space to get practice!

> PRACTICE GENERALLY DOESN'T PAY WELL, IT USUALLY ISN'T GLAMOROUS, AND THOSE REPS DON'T COME WITH A CORNER OFFICE.

And keep in mind, practice generally doesn't pay well, it usually isn't glamorous, and those reps don't come with a corner office. It requires discipline, passion, and a commitment to your craft to work through this stage of your journey, not to mention setting aside pride and fear. But once you get experience and begin to build your skill set, you're going to start seeing your hard work pay off with opportunities and open doors. Then you'll be ready to start looking toward the next stage of the climb: finding a place to perform!

THE PROXIMITY PROCESS

1. Make a list of companies or organizations you would love to work for.

2. Research whether these places offer internships or accept volunteers.

3. Determine how your skills could add value to those around you, then make a list of ways you can get experience by offering your services for free.

CHAPTER 10

A PLACE TO PERFORM

The only way to do great work is to love what you do. If you haven't found it yet, keep looking. And don't settle. As with all matters of the heart, you'll know when you find it.

—STEVE JOBS

If you've ever closely followed comedians and musicians, you've likely heard them talk about doing college tours when they were starting out. Some of these experiences are pretty hilarious, even though they were often miserable for these folks! They would sometimes have to drive hundreds of miles in one day to get from one university gig to the next, and they'd never quite know what to expect when they'd arrive. There are hilarious stories of musicians and comedians showing up at one campus for an outdoor show in snow flurries for eight people and then driving twelve hours overnight to show up the next day in the corner of a college cafeteria during parent weekend!

Emmy Award-winning comedian Sara Schaefer told of some of her experiences: "One time, a school insisted on dramatically raising me up out of an orchestra pit through a cloud of smoke. . . . Another time, it was just me in an almost empty student lounge trying to shout over the blaring TVs (because the moody student assigned to me 'didn't know' how to turn them off). I've pretty much seen it all."[43] Most of the time, these types of gigs are less than ideal, the tour schedules are grueling, the pay is lousy, and the audiences are less than attentive. But the interesting thing is, there's a lot of competition to get hired for these spots. These performers will do almost anything to get in front of a live audience.

I've noticed the same thing about the aspiring musicians I've met since moving to Nashville. They are always performing. Always. They play in half-empty clubs, in airports, in coffee shops, wherever they can get a paid gig. The question is, *Why*? They do this because they know even the most talented musicians don't walk into a record label and sign a contract. Musicians and comedians know the importance of stepping in front of a live audience to put all that practice and talent to the test. In fact, their future in entertainment depends on it.

Comedians and musicians know that more can be gained from one hour on stage than five in the studio. A live audience isn't always accepting or forgiving. When these performers are in the middle of a song or set, they can feel how the crowd is responding in real time. They learn to watch for cues and adjust their material to keep the audience's attention. Comedians like Pete Holmes, who now has his own HBO show, and musicians like the three-time Grammy Award–nominated band The Avett Brothers spent time in these places before making it big. No matter the field, most successful professionals started small and refined their craft in their place to perform.

EMBRACING THE ENTRY LEVEL

When you're in your place to perform, it comes with the reality that you're starting in the minor leagues— you probably won't be sitting in a corner office, the pay isn't going to be great, and you're going to have to work really hard. Beth Comstock, the former chief marketing officer and vice chair for innovation at GE, first worked at a Rubbermaid factory, and she admits that she didn't think she was cut out for it at first. "I was working with injection molding machines that produced spatulas, beer mugs, and huge trash bins. This wasn't the *I Love Lucy* chocolate factory job; it was hot and the pace was intense."[44] That experience shaped her work ethic and determination. In 2015 Comstock was named one of "The World's 100 Most Powerful Women" by Forbes. In 2017, just a few months before leaving GE, she said her advice to young professionals is to relax a little when it comes to those entry-level positions: "I usually tell them their first job doesn't determine their life. People often put too much pressure on that first job. Just try things out. Sometimes the seemingly worst assignments can be your best. What are you going to bring to it? What are you going to learn from it?"[45]

As you get in closer proximity to your dream job, don't fall into the trap of seeing entry-level work as a necessary evil. Your place to perform should be in your chosen industry, but it doesn't need to be the *exact* type of work you want to be doing. Sometimes the job won't be fun, or the audience won't be as big as you'd like. That's when taking Comstock's advice is your best play. *What are you going to bring to it?* Give each moment your all and know that all those little moments add up and impact your career. You're learning from the professionals you work alongside and from the producers who have given you this opportunity. You're being paid to do work you care about, you're learning and growing, and you're making a difference to your employer's bottom line—these are the characteristics of entry-level work that should be celebrated. The value you bring isn't going to go unnoticed! So embrace these positions in all their powerful potential, because they will push you to the next stage in your climb!

WHAT YOU STAND TO GAIN

Your place to perform might not be ideal, but it should always be in the field you want to be in with people doing what you want to do. This is where you'll learn what it means to be a professional. You've simply got to show up, give it 100 percent, and add value to the people you work with and the place you work for. When you do, you'll learn or gain three things to help you on your climb:

1. How to Handle Pressure
2. When to Pivot
3. Confirmation

I believe we're all created to do specific work in our lives, and the place to perform is where you start actually leaning into what you're created to do. You'll learn and grow with real-world experience, and you'll get confirmation that this is exactly where you need to be.

How to Handle Pressure

Handling pressure is a skill that comes with time and experience. Sometimes the ability to perform under pressure is what separates the practicers from the performers. Athletes, in particular, get a lot of attention for high-pressure performance. Runners will tell you that there is a big difference between training and an actual race where you can feel people watching on the sidelines and the other runners at your heels. And Olympic athletes carry an intense amount of pressure when they compete. Learning to deal with it is even part of their training. Look at Gabby Douglas, for instance. She was part of the 2016 Summer Olympics girls' gymnastics team and has not one, but *three* gold medals. When asked how she handles pressure, Douglas answered, "For the most part, I'm kind of used to it, because it has been a part of me for my whole life. I'm trained to deal under those circumstances." For Douglas, that training looked like "pressure sets," where a gymnast pretends she is in competition and doesn't let anything slide.[46]

> THE PLACE TO PERFORM IS WHERE YOU START ACTUALLY LEANING INTO WHAT YOU'RE CREATED TO DO.

And then there's Michael Phelps, who has won more gold medals than any other Olympic athlete ever—twenty-three to be exact. He explained that part of dealing with pressure is training for it: "I think to perform under pressure, obviously, you have to prepare. . . . Also I think you really just have to be focused. You know, in a big spot when the lights are turned on, there are so many people who get distracted from 'x-y-z' and they're not focused on exactly what they want to do and what they're trying to accomplish."[47]

The first time I sat down to do my very own radio

show and that microphone went hot, it was no longer practice time. It was my first broadcasting situation, and the pressure was on to perform. Producers at the station had advertising to sell, and they expected me to put on a good show. It was live radio with real people listening. Up to this point, I had done sports play-by-play, volunteered at a radio station, and sat behind the mic before, but this was different because it was my very own show: *The Ken Coleman Show*. The amount of pressure I was experiencing now was much different from what I had experienced before. It was clear to me that I had reached a different place in my climb up the mountain. And while I was so excited to have made it this far, the stakes were much higher from this vantage point.

When to Pivot

There's little room for error on live radio. Calls can take unpredictable turns quickly, and I had to learn when to pivot. Discerning when to transition to another topic when things weren't going well and managing problems in the middle of an interview are not things you can practice in advance. It's on-the-job training at its best. And while you may never have to manage this on air, you will most certainly have to do this in your place to perform. It's a problem-solving skill that's absolutely critical as you climb your mountain.

Brian's place to perform was on Broadway. But not in the way you might guess. He worked as a theatrical sound engineer and he called our show one day to talk about how he learned the art of pivoting. Brian had gotten a job at a prominent theater in Philadelphia. But despite all of the practice he'd had (even in dress rehearsals), he couldn't truly prepare himself for the real, live performance of opening night. He learned more that first night about the nuances of prepping the soundboards and adjusting the microphones on the fly than he ever had in rehearsals. He was forced to

KNOWING WHEN TO PIVOT IS A PROBLEM-SOLVING SKILL THAT'S ABSOLUTELY CRITICAL.

troubleshoot problems very quickly, pushing and pulling faders to balance the sound and making sure each sound had its own space. This ability to pivot quickly gave Brian a skill set that made him valuable to the theater and that could separate him from other engineers.

Confirmation

If anyone ever found some of the early tapes from *The Ken Coleman Show*, I would be pretty embarrassed at how unpolished they sound. But I also think back fondly to that time of my career. I was working my tail off, doing a ton of preparation for each week, and loving every minute of it! Sure, I felt nervous about being live and the pressure of coming up with the program. But I also felt the exhilaration of performing as soon as the mic turned on and a ton of satisfaction when each show was done. That little one-hour show on Saturdays confirmed that I was in exactly the right field because there was no amount of hard work that could discourage me from it. Did I want to do a one-hour local radio show for the rest of my career? No! I wanted to climb higher! The podcast of the show was growing, and feedback was coming in from the station and listeners. All of this only added to my desire to press on toward my goal of having a national show and making a career out of broadcasting.

And the same will be true for you. The gains you'll see while you are working in your place to perform will push and drive you to climb faster and harder up the mountain. You will learn how to handle high-pressure situations, you'll learn how and when to pivot using problem-solving techniques, and you'll get the confirmation you need to know you are pursuing the *right* dream!

FINDING YOUR PLACE TO PERFORM

In order to find places to perform, think about where you've been learning and practicing. Who might benefit from all the knowledge you've gained and skills you've sharpened? Keep your eyes open for producers who are maxed out, overworked, or in need of extra help. How might you step in to add value to their business or operation?

For example, Katie, a woman who called into the show one day, wanted to transition from her publicity role to an events management career. She began to do some research and started learning the skills she'd need for a job. Then a local nonprofit announced they needed volunteers for their big, annual fundraiser. Katie jumped at this opportunity. While she was working at the event, the event coordinator said that she'd taken an in-house, paid position with the nonprofit. The problem was, they didn't know how to handle the soon-to-be vacant event coordinator spot. Katie happily offered to step into that entry-level position to help ease the transition on a temporary basis. That pleased the producer and allowed Katie the chance to perform—even if not yet in a paid role.

A place to perform is a vital step toward getting that job you've dreamed about. It's the space where you really begin to grasp the attitude, effort, and aptitude to turn pro. And it's the place you finally get to put your skill set to work and move closer to the summit. Then, once you've embraced what it means to perform well in your field, you'll be ready for the final and most exciting stage of your journey: finding a place to grow.

THE PROXIMITY PROCESS

1. Research local and national entry-level opportunities in your field.

2. Determine which of those opportunities are a "yes" to the following questions:

   ▸ Will it give you real and relevant experience in the field you want to be in?

   ▸ Does it offer the chance for you to win under pressure?

   ▸ Will you be able to add value to the producers in the company or organization?

CHAPTER 11

A PLACE TO GROW

Without continual growth and progress,
such words as improvement, achievement,
and success have no meaning.

—BENJAMIN FRANKLIN

J. D. Henigman started working for a medical distribution company shortly after graduating high school. But after several years working in the warehousing and logistics field, it was clear that there was not room to grow there. So he left. Henigman wasn't going to let the absence of opportunity stop him on his way to the top so he took a position at Graybar, a company that focuses on employee growth.[48] Several years and *promotions* later, Henigman serves as the branch manager at the Evansville, Indiana, location. He's in charge of recruiting and hiring, and for him that includes helping his team grow in their careers: "When you're recruiting and hiring, some things are negotiable—like salary and benefits, but when you can present an environment that centers both on organizational success and individual success, you wind up with a winning formula."[49] J. D. Henigman understands how important it is for companies to offer their employees opportunities to grow, and now he is doing exactly what led him to his company in the first place: making sure everyone finds a role that is a good fit for them and helping them grow in it.

IT'S GROW TIME

At this stage in your climb, all of the elements of The Proximity Principle will start coming together. But finding a place to grow will take some time, intention, and discernment. Look for places where there are clear opportunities for you to develop and maximize all of your strengths and talents for the organization. That's how you'll begin to advance your career. And you should be open to changing zip codes in this phase. Now's the

IN YOUR PLACE TO GROW, ALL OF THE ELEMENTS OF THE PROXIMITY PRINCIPLE WILL START COMING TOGETHER.

time to seize opportunities you've always dreamed about and worked tirelessly to claim!

Where to Grow

Caitlin always knew that she wanted to be an in-house editor. She loved books and had a passion for working with talented writers. In order to get there, she started out in an entry-level position with a small publisher. She worked her way up through the stages of learning and practicing until she was performing as the managing editor at a small fiction publisher. Caitlin understood that getting in proximity to her dream job might require a move to a larger publishing house, but she was willing to do that if she found the right place. She began turning over rocks and found an opening at an international publishing house in New York City. The opportunity sounded good, but before she was willing to make the move, she needed to do some research. It was time to dig in.

As she learned more about the company, Caitlin discovered that their core mission and values aligned with her own. Second, she believed in the quality of authors they signed and the way the company treated them. And finally, she was impressed with the vision and talent of the people she'd be working with at the company and the way the company took care of their employees. In fact, many of the people at the publishing house were considered the best in the business. This got her excited! Based on that knowledge, she knew she'd be ready to make the move to New York City if she got the job.

During the interview process, Caitlin met with the publisher and CEO of the organization. She felt challenged and supported when they talked through her career goal of working in book acquisitions. If she excelled in the editorial role, there would be a clear path forward leading her to the long-term role that she wanted. The opportunity for growth was there, and she knew exactly what was expected to get in closer proximity to her dream job. When Caitlin landed the job, she was completely confident it was the right move for her to grow in her career.

THREE MUST-HAVES IN A PLACE TO GROW

Caitlin saw three key elements at the New York publishing house that we should all look for in our own place to grow:

1. Alignment of Values
2. A Healthy Challenge
3. A Clear Path Forward

No matter what area you want to work in or how big or small the company, you should look for a place that shares your same values, provides a healthy challenge, and offers a clear path forward. These three things will keep you motivated in your place to grow and will advance your career and push you higher up your mountain.

Alignment of Values

If you find a company you're interested in, do your homework. Take the time to carefully investigate their core mission. These days most companies are transparent and clear with their mission statement and values—often they even list these things on their website. Do some discovery and ask yourself this question: *Do my personal values line up with the company's core mission?* If there's tension between what you stand for and what the company values, beware. You want to do work that matters and gives you joy. If you're working for a company that has a core mission you don't believe in, you won't be happy for long, even if the role you're in gets you closer to your dream job. It's hard to grow professionally when you're personally conflicted. If the culture of a place is unhealthy, you might start thinking you should be doing something else, when, in reality, you are doing the right work, just in the wrong place. In this case, you simply need to change places, not careers. But when you find a place where your core values align with your employer's, that will give you the foundation to truly grow as a professional.

Shannon is a great example of how important the alignment of values can be for your growth. Shannon was passionate about helping nonprofit organizations.

Her dream was to run a marketing firm that focused on supporting nonprofits and charities. She found her place to perform as the marketing manager at a local advertising firm, which gave her actual experience in working on campaigns for car dealerships, law firms, and commercial real estate. While this gave Shannon the confirmation she needed to know she was in the right industry, the work just wasn't fulfilling. She longed to use her marketing skills to serve her community and impact the lives of people in need.

IT'S HARD TO GROW PROFESSIONALLY WHEN YOU'RE PERSONALLY CONFLICTED.

After a good deal of interviewing and searching for the right situation, she accepted a position at a prominent marketing firm that served food banks, homeless shelters, and international missions. Six years later Shannon became the CEO of that marketing firm! Because their core mission aligned with Shannon's own core mission, she was passionate about the work she was doing which accelerated her professional growth. When you're passionate about your job because you believe in what you're doing, you'll care more and you'll put more into it. The results will matter to you, so you'll strive for excellence. In turn, you'll find yourself on the fast-track to career growth in a place that aligns with your values. And that's a great place to be!

A Healthy Challenge

The second key to growing as a professional is surrounding yourself with high-achieving peers who perform with excellence and challenge you to do the same. The 1992 USA Olympic Basketball team—known as the Dream Team—understood this well. The Dream Team is arguably the greatest collection of basketball players in history. The roster was made up of big names like Michael Jordan, Larry Bird, Magic Johnson, Karl Malone, Charles Barkley, and John Stockton. The Dream Team beat its Olympic opponents by a ridiculous average of almost forty-four points a game. It was an incredible thing to see.

But what was even more incredible than that was "The Greatest Game Nobody Ever Saw," the nickname given to a legendary practice scrimmage before the actual Olympic games were played. Team USA vs. Team USA. Team Blue vs. Team White. Team Blue was led by Magic Johnson and included Charles Barkley, David Robinson, Chris Mullin, and Christian Laettner. And Team White was led by Michael Jordan and included Karl Malone, Patrick Ewing, Scottie Pippen, and Larry Bird. Behind closed doors these guys

YOU WILL EXPERIENCE THE MOST GROWTH WHEN YOU SURROUND YOURSELF WITH TALENTED PEOPLE WHO CHALLENGE YOU TO PERFORM AT A HIGHER LEVEL.

had something to prove—not to the world, because the world wasn't watching—but to *themselves*. They were *all* the best of the best, so they challenged and pushed each other to an even higher level of excellence.[50]

Occasionally I talk with people on my show who say they want to become the all-star employee at their company. And I have to tell them that while it's great that they want to work hard and excel at their company, focusing on being the all-star can actually limit their growth. The truth is you will experience the most growth when you surround yourself with talented and hardworking people who consistently challenge you to perform at a higher level. This is the kind of attitude and mind-set that put the "dream" in the Dream Team. They weren't out there trying to get recognition for themselves. They were working together to win for the team. And that's what you should do in your own place to grow.

A Clear Path Forward

The third and final key element you should look for in your place to grow is a clear path forward. My friend Sean was able to find this in a teaching role. Sean loved the idea of inspiring young writers as an English professor at a university. So after finishing his graduate work, he got to work researching which universities would give him the best chance at a coveted full-time teaching position. He interviewed with several department chairs at local colleges. Then he further narrowed his search by determining which universities had professors close to retirement and which had growing enrollments. Sean's research and discovery paid off. He knew he couldn't just step into his dream job full time, so he accepted a role as an adjunct professor at a university in Pittsburg that showed opportunity for a clear path forward.

Sean's adjunct position got him in proximity to the position he really wanted, and he used the part-time gig as a place to grow. He spent the next two years teaching the classes that no one else wanted to teach—at the hours no one else wanted to teach them—while earning just enough to pay his bills. Even as an adjunct professor, he was able to quickly establish himself as an influential instructor, which then earned him a full-time position. Several years later Sean became tenured and he continues to grow and push himself in his career. His next goal is to become the department chair. Sean put in the time and energy to find a place with a clear path for advancement, and then he performed at a high level to get in proximity to his dream job.

Finding a place to grow that aligns with your values, challenges and pushes you to become better, and offers a clear path forward will help advance your career in ways you never imagined possible. Don't get discouraged if when you start looking the first few places don't have one or two of these key elements. Keep at it! Keep turning over rocks and doing your research. Companies like this do exist. And they are looking for people just like you to join their team!

FINDING YOUR PLACE TO GROW

When I look back on my own journey, it's clear that my leap from Atlanta to Nashville to work for Dave Ramsey gave me the perfect place to grow. I'd discovered my places to learn—with education and jobs where I learned the fundamentals of broadcasting. I'd found my places to practice—taking unpaid gigs like calling high school football games. And I'd had great opportunities in my places to perform—hosting events and my own radio show. Now Ramsey Solutions was my place to grow.

I changed my zip code for three reasons. First, I wanted to do the kind of work that would change people's lives and give them hope. That is the focus of Dave's company, so I knew the core mission and values of Ramsey Solutions aligned with my own. Second, I wanted to be challenged to grow by the excellent people I worked with. Dave already had a team of some of the most talented professionals I could imagine, so I knew I'd be surrounded by a "dream team" that would push me to raise my game and perform at my best. And third, I wanted to work somewhere with a clear path forward. I knew that if I came to work for Dave and busted my butt with a great attitude, growth would eventually come. Choosing to work with Ramsey

Solutions continues to be one of the greatest professional decisions I've ever made. And I want you to have that same experience.

If you are faithful about walking through each stage of the process and you're willing to put The Proximity Principle to work, you will naturally build the foundation of success that will lead you to your place to grow. Then it will be time to implement some strategies and practices to finish your climb and reach the summit.

THE PROXIMITY PROCESS

1. Write down the values and type of work culture that matters deeply to you.

2. Make a list of the companies that have your dream job whose core mission, values, and culture matches what matters to you.

3. Determine whether those companies have a clear path forward.

PART 3

THE PRACTICES

*A dream doesn't become reality
through magic; it takes sweat,
determination, and hard work.*

—COLIN POWELL

In 1988 Nike launched a new marketing campaign with the slogan "Just Do It." What few people know is that when the idea was initially pitched by the advertising agency, everyone at Nike hated it. When they ran with it anyway, it became huge. Most importantly that decision was a major turning point for the brand. "Just Do It" became Nike's signature slogan and is now virtually synonymous with the brand. The phrase helped boost sales for the company which, at the time, was struggling to keep up with Reebok, and now, over thirty years later, the slogan is still as strong as ever.

> THIS COULD BE YOUR MOMENT. STOP *DREAMING* ABOUT IT AND START *DOING* SOMETHING ABOUT IT.

But why? Why did the slogan "Just Do It" resonate so strongly with people? I think it's because the message is so simple.[51] It says, "No more excuses." No more excuses for not seeing the results you want. No more excuses for not getting up and getting moving. No more excuses for not pushing yourself to where you want to be. No more excuses for not winning. This is the mind-set you have to adopt if you want The Proximity Principle to work for you! No more excuses.

In the first two parts of this book, I've shown you *who* you need to be around and *where* you need to put yourself. That's The Proximity Principle. It's tried and true. It works if you do. You've just got to do it. You have to step out before you can step up. Then you keep stepping until you step into your dream job. But you've got to decide. You have to put your stake in the ground and do something to make it happen. This could be your moment. Stop *dreaming* about it and start *doing* something about it.

Now, in the last section of the book, we are going to talk about what you need to do *after* you've identified the right people and places. In this stage, you'll do four specific things that I call "The Proximity Practices." These are essential to helping you finish your climb to the summit. You'll work on:

1. Creating a Web of Connections
2. Making Your Connections Count
3. Seizing the Opportunity
4. Adopting a Proximity Mind-set

Ready? Let's do this.

CHAPTER 12

CREATING A WEB OF CONNECTIONS

*Pulling a good network together
takes effort, sincerity and time.*

—ALAN COLLINS

Think back to when you were sixteen years old and needed gas money. Unless you were super lucky, your parents probably pushed you out the front door to go find your very first job. And I'd venture to guess getting that first job wasn't very hard. The process was pretty straightforward. More than likely, someone you already knew connected you to a producer, a person who could give you a job. Maybe you asked your friends at school, on your team, or at church about how to get hired at the restaurant or the grocery store. Or your parents asked their friends if they were hiring. Or you may have even walked into a store and talked to the manager because you knew a few people who worked there.

The point is you didn't need a resumé. I highly doubt you used LinkedIn. And I'm almost certain that you didn't attend a networking event! You used your *connections* to find that first job. That simple approach worked for you when you were sixteen, and the truth is: that same approach will work for you today. Creating a web of connections—having purposeful interactions with people who are in the place you want to be—is the first action item you'll need to do to get you closer to your dream job.

STOP SPEED NETWORKING

I'm all about making valuable connections with people and helping others get to where they want to be in their career, but traditional networking events are not an effective venue for making worthwhile connections. These events are designed to give job seekers the opportunity to meet business professionals in the hopes that you will hit it off and make such a great first impression that it will lead to a job interview. It's like speed dating for business.

The last time I ever attended a networking event I felt like I'd walked into a meat market. I'd been there for several minutes when a guy came up to me bouncing with so much energy, it was like he was a human version of Tigger from *Winnie the Pooh*. I was honestly kind of taken aback at how aggressively interested he was in talking to me. This guy made me feel like a million bucks—at first. We exchanged hellos and started with the obligatory small talk that's expected at these events: "What do you do for a living? Where do you work? . . . etc." And I mean in no less than forty-five seconds he went from full-on stalker mode to completely ignoring me as he scanned over my shoulder for his next victim. As soon as he realized that I was in an industry that was of zero benefit to him, he checked out.

USE THE CONNECTIONS YOU ALREADY HAVE TO MAKE NEW ONES IN THE PLACE YOU'D LOVE TO WORK.

Believe me, your time and energy are too precious to spend at these types of events. In fact, I'm giving you permission to *never* attend another traditional networking event for the rest of your life! They're awful. They rarely lead to a genuine connection with the right people to help you land your dream job. Instead, use the connections you already have to make new ones in the place you'd love to work.

EXPAND YOUR CIRCLE

Earlier in the People section I said, It's not just *what* you know, it's *who* you know! There's a lot of truth in that statement, but when it comes to connecting to job opportunities, most of the time it's not just who *you* know, it's who *they* know. Getting that first job as a teenager was quite a bit easier than getting in proximity to your dream job as an adult. Why? Because younger people tend to stick to their inner circle of family and friends to connect them to a job—any job that puts gas in the gas tank. But the reality is, your chances of getting a job that you really want are much higher if you step outside of your inner circle and connect with people you don't know as well. The people *they* know. Your *outer* circle.

Mark Granovetter is a sociology professor at Stanford University. His main focus of study has been the interactions of social networks. In his article "The Strength of Weak Ties," which was published in *The American Journal of Sociology*, Granovetter used the term *weak ties* to describe people who aren't in your inner circle. His research shows that connecting with these weak ties leads to more opportunity. In fact, he says that people were 58 percent more likely to get a job through weak ties than through strong ones.[52] And it makes a lot of sense. If you rely only on the people in your inner circle to connect you to job opportunities, then you're limited to a pretty small job pool. But if you expand your circle to include weak ties—who *they* know—the pool gets a whole lot bigger. It's kind of like playing the Six Degrees of Kevin Bacon game. I know it's a crazy analogy, but stick with me for a minute.

Learning from Kevin Bacon

The game is based on the "six degrees of separation" theory—the idea is that any two people in the world can be connected through six or fewer acquaintances. In Six Degrees of Kevin Bacon, players challenge each other to find the shortest path between Kevin Bacon and another Hollywood actor. For instance, if you and I were playing the game, I would throw out an actor's name like Melissa McCarthy. Your job would be to connect Melissa McCarthy to Kevin Bacon. So you might remember that McCarthy was in the movie *Bridesmaids* with Kristen Wiig. You'd then connect Kristen Wiig to Steve Carell because they were in *Date Night* together. Finally, you would connect Steve Carell to the movie *Crazy, Stupid, Love* with none other than . . . Kevin Bacon. Bam! Within three movies—three degrees of separation—you arrived at Kevin Bacon. It's a pretty fun game to pass time on car trips. But how does this game and the theory of six degrees of separation apply to The Proximity Principle? With a method I like to call "Creating a Web of Connections."

Creating a Web of Connections

When I use the word *web*, I'm sure the image of a spider web immediately pops into your mind. And that's exactly

CREATING A WEB OF CONNECTIONS IS THE BEST WAY TO GET THE OPPORTUNITIES YOU REALLY WANT. what I'm going for here. Spiders are remarkable creatures, and their webs are equally fascinating. If you've ever been lucky enough to see a spider web in the morning light, covered in dew, you get what I'm saying. Their webs are intricate and very, very strong.

William K. Purves, a biology professor, explained just how strong dragline silk, a specific type of silk spun by spiders, is in an article he wrote for *Scientific American*:

> Dragline silk combines toughness and strength to an extraordinary degree. A dragline strand is several times stronger than steel, on a weight-for-weight basis, but a spider's dragline is only about one-tenth the diameter of a human hair. The movie *Spider-Man* drastically underestimates the strength of silk. Real dragline silk would not need to be nearly as thick as the strands deployed by our web-swinging hero in the movie.[53]

Okay, so you might be thinking, *Thanks for the biology lesson, but how will this get me in proximity to my dream job?* Creating your own web of connections using a strong network of people—similar to how a spider spins an incredibly strong web to catch its next meal—is the best way to get the opportunities you really want. This web will be made up of your inner circle of people—your close friends and family—who are then connected to an outer circle of people who can connect you to the work you want to do. So to create a web strong enough to get the results you want, you just need to follow three simple steps. Then you can sit back and watch opportunities find you. You should:

1. Inform Your Inner Circle
2. Create a Connection To-do List
3. Connect with the People on Your List

Let's go a little deeper on each of these steps.

Inform Your Inner Circle

The process of creating a web of connections starts by sharing your dream with your inner circle of close family and friends. These are the people you care about most and who care about you the most. So tell them exactly what you want to do and where you want to go. Then ask them to think of people they know or places they have access to that they are willing to connect you to. They will start thinking through their own web of connections to find anyone they know who could possibly help you. The close relationships and acquaintances they have are potential connections to get you to your dream job.

Create a Connection To-do List

Once you have a list of connections from your inner circle, it's your turn to sit down, think through your own acquaintances, and make a list of those connections. You may want to create "buckets," or categories, to help you identify all of your contacts based on how you know them. Buckets could include former coworkers, former classmates, people you've met at social clubs, and neighbors. Debbie recently called my show and said she hardly knew anybody outside of her family and close friends. I took a shot in the dark and asked, "Do you have kids?" She said, "Three." I then asked if they played sports. She chuckled as she told me how busy her family is with the kids' sports schedules. I asked Debbie if she had developed friendships with any of the other moms from her kids' teams. I could hear the light bulb turn on in her head as she paused and said, "I sure have." She knew what I was going to ask next. Debbie knew more people than she thought she did. Every one of those moms is an acquaintance and a connection, and the opportunity she is looking for could be sitting on the bleachers with her every week.

Connect with the People on Your List

With a little intentionality and thought, you will have a list with plenty of connections you need to make. Once you've reviewed, researched, and prioritized your list of people and places, ask your inner circle or other contacts to connect you to those people in your outer circle. I know this can feel really intimidating, but the truth is that parts of this process are going to feel a little uncomfortable. And that's okay! Connecting with people you hardly know doesn't have to happen in an awkward phone call or in a formal meeting in an office. It can be really laid back—over coffee or lunch. The important thing is that it's an actual conversation. Don't try to have a conversation through email. Sit with these folks face-to-face. Then just like you did with your inner circle, tell them what your Mount Everest is and ask them if they know of any opportunities or have connections with any relevant people.

HOW IT WORKED FOR ME

Now listen, I know this seems like a lot of work just to get a few connections, but I can promise you, these three simple steps work! I know it works because when I first started thinking about how to get into broadcasting, I didn't use this method. And I ran into a wall. I got nowhere. When I decided to take my first step into broadcasting I thought I'd cold-call a manager of a local radio station in Georgia. When he didn't return my call the first time, I called again. And again. I just knew this manager could help me get my own show. But I didn't know him personally. Looking back on it, I'm sure he thought I was a complete lunatic . . . and a determined one at that. It's no wonder why he didn't respond to my messages. Since leaving messages wasn't working, I had to come up with a new strategy. So I sat down and started creating a web of connections. I brainstormed my contacts and wrote down all the people I knew. And let me just tell you, I'm not a natural list maker, but I wanted to find just one connection to that manager.

As I went through the names I'd come up with, one name in particular stuck out: Elizabeth. Something pinged in my brain as I remembered meeting with her months earlier as a favor to a mutual friend. He connected us because Elizabeth wanted some advice on getting sponsorships for a nonprofit she was working with. And because my wife Stacy and I had our own sponsorship sales company and did this on a contract basis for several organizations, my friend knew I could help out his friend. At the time, I was hosting a highly successful podcast for a leadership conference, and when Elizabeth and I were talking, she told me she'd listened in and enjoyed it. In passing, she mentioned that her family owned a radio station. I remembered that piece of information from talking to her and was now wondering if Elizabeth was connected to the *very* station where I'd been leaving messages for the manager.

I called Elizabeth that morning and told her my dream was to do radio. I explained that I had an idea for a show, but I hadn't been able to connect with the general manager. She told me her brother was none other than the CEO of the radio station, and I had to pick my jaw up off the floor. I couldn't believe it! Elizabeth said she'd connect us, and just one week later, I was sitting in his office! Just one week after sitting down with my list of connections, I was pitching the CEO of the radio station my idea of a weekly show. Long story short, he liked my idea and said he'd give it a chance. Then he slotted me for Saturdays. And that was how the very first version of *The Ken Coleman Show* came to be. So a connection I made as a favor to a friend returned itself to me many months later as one of the biggest breaks of my career— all because I took the time to create a web of connections.

A WORTHY INVESTMENT

When you take the time and energy to work through this step, you'll create a strong network of people who can help you reach the next level of your climb. Don't think you can skip it and get there on your own. You can't. The connections you make with people are critical to getting you where you want to be. And don't become overwhelmed by the process. If you'll just sit down and make a list of all the people you know, you'll realize you're already closer than you thought to the people who can help you. Put aside the fear of rejection and remember that you're only asking people for a connection. If you hit a dead

> MAKE A LIST OF ALL YOUR CONNECTIONS, AND YOU'LL REALIZE YOU'RE ALREADY CLOSER THAN YOU THOUGHT TO THE PEOPLE WHO CAN HELP YOU.

end in one circle of friends, just move on to the next one on your list. Occasionally you can catch lightning in a bottle and one or two meetings could put you in a great place. But more often than not, this takes time. Stick with it. The practice of making new connections, meeting new professionals and producers, and then learning from these pros is so important to catching opportunities. You're investing to get closer to work that matters to you! I've benefitted from using this approach over and over in my career, and I'm certain it can work for you.

CHAPTER 13

MAKING YOUR CONNECTIONS COUNT

People will forget what you said. People will forget what you did. But people will never forget how you made them feel.

—MAYA ANGELOU

Now that you know how to get connected to people, let's focus on how to approach those connections the right way. Remember, there are five groups of people you need to build relationships with:

Professors teach you the basics.
Professionals model the way.

Mentors provide wisdom and accountability.
Peers push you toward excellence.
Producers give you opportunities.

Real relationships cannot be manufactured or artificially mass-produced. They take time and intention if they're going to grow. Like with everything else, the more you put into your relationships, the more impactful they can be.

As you are looking for opportunities through your connections, ask yourself two questions:

1. Where can I learn?
2. Where can I get experience?

Answering these questions will move you into proximity to the people who can help you. But here's something you need to know: you're going to have to boldly outwork everyone else. Why? Because like I said at the beginning of this book, no one is spending their time thinking about how they can help you get to your dream job. So as you begin making connections, think about the 250 resumés that arrive in the inbox of hiring managers for every job. I'm telling you, the competition is fierce!

> REAL RELATIONSHIPS CANNOT BE MANUFACTURED OR ARTIFICIALLY MASS-PRODUCED.

BE BOLD AND AUDACIOUS,
BUT NOT OBNOXIOUS

Here's what I want you to tell yourself in order to maintain your edge: *Everyday there are people out there working harder than me to get the job I want.* It's up to you to put in the effort to get where you want to be! No matter what opportunities come your way, you should treat them like a job, do your work as if people are watching, always give it your best effort, and understand that no task is beneath you. My advice is to be *bold* and *audacious* without being *obnoxious*. It's like the young James Farmer Jr. says in one of my favorite movies, *The Great Debaters*: "We do what we got to do, so we can do what we want to." Get ready to do what it takes!

Be Bold

The truth is that putting yourself out there and boldly working through The Proximity Principle isn't easy. If it was, everyone would be doing it. Far too many people are too timid when going after their dream job. Opportunities pass by, and sometimes, after identifying the right people, those limiting beliefs of fear or pride stop us in our tracks. Don't let your limiting beliefs keep you from taking bold steps toward your dream. What does this mean practically? It means this: to overcome fear and pride, you have to put yourself out there and do whatever it takes to prove yourself. Don't worry about appearing too aggressive. There are ways to keep that in check.

Be Audacious

Audacious isn't a word we use very often, but I like it—and especially in this context. Merriam-Webster defines it as "intrepidly daring" and "recklessly bold."[54] Being audacious about pursuing your dream job means you're driven by courage and conviction. You are bold and confident, but at the same time, you maintain a posture of humility. You understand your need for others, and you genuinely want to learn from them. If you approach people with this kind of hungry and humble mind-set, people will never mistake your audacity for aggression.

Being audacious also means you bring value to the connections and relationships you build instead of solely approaching them from a transactional standpoint. I remember finding a Zig Ziglar quote as a senior in high school that changed my whole outlook on this idea. It says: "You can get everything in life you want if you will just help enough other people get what they want." It's no wonder that statement stuck with me all these years! That kind of thinking is so counter to what we are used to hearing from culture, but, man, shouldn't we all want to live that way?

Kaleb, a caller to my show, is a great example of this Ziglar principle. Kaleb worked in pharmaceutical sales but wanted to transition to selling medical devices. He identified a few of the companies that he hoped to work for, created a web of connections, and found some producers he wanted to meet with. One of those producers was a local sales manager named Russ. Kaleb wanted to spend some time talking with Russ about different sales tactics specific to both industries, but he hadn't had the chance to

BEING AUDACIOUS ABOUT PURSUING YOUR DREAM JOB MEANS YOU'RE DRIVEN BY COURAGE AND CONVICTION.

touch base in several weeks. The mutual friend that helped connect Kaleb to Russ had mentioned that Russ was a huge hockey fan, so Kaleb was bold enough to buy some game tickets. Kaleb called the show right after he purchased the tickets so I'm not sure how this turned out. But I thought it was a creative way for Kaleb to connect and show he wasn't just in it for what he could get out of Russ.

Don't Be Obnoxious

Everyone has that one person they think of when they hear the word *obnoxious.* Am I right? You're thinking of some annoying person right now, aren't you? Well, for our purposes—climbing Mount Everest—I like to think of obnoxious behavior as audacity without humility and self-awareness. These people are pushy and braggy.

Some people are obnoxious because they're schmoozers. You know the type. Everyone they work with knows they didn't get their job or the big promotion based on performance, but they sure act like they did. They're brown-nosers. Name-droppers. When they talk, there may be quite a few eyerolls from others in the room. Schmoozers don't recognize that time and relationships are extremely valuable. They're in it for themselves and can turn people off with their aggressive personalities.

Other people are obnoxious because their passion is on overdrive. They're so focused on the path ahead that they unintentionally bulldoze everyone on it. I truly believe that these people are completely unaware of how their behavior affects those around them. They're just on full throttle and have a really hard time taking it down a notch.

As painful and embarrassing as it is to admit, early on in my climb to a broadcasting career, I was a classic case of this. I was so hyper-focused on my goals that I would accelerate from zero to sixty as quickly as possible, even when meeting with key people who could open doors of opportunity for me. I wanted to learn as much as I could so badly that sometimes I wasn't patient enough to really listen. I wanted to push past their questions and get right to the opportunity. Some people appreciated my enthusiasm, but many times I came on way too strong.

I once had the chance to meet with a regional personality for Turner Sports. I was trying to get an entry-level TV gig, and in order to get an on-camera role, I needed a demo of myself. This guy was a pretty big deal and was kind enough to offer his help. I was extremely grateful that he took the time to teach me some tricks, like how to read a teleprompter and how to announce sports highlights. And I was humbled that he was giving me a chance to sit behind the desk and practice doing the highlights. But let me tell you, that's not what my behavior indicated. I got to the studio before his show, and as we talked, my passion and a whole lot of words just spewed out of me—and all over him. And not in a good way. At the time, I had no real experience, but that didn't stop me from serial name-dropping and trying to impress him with my accomplishments. To make matters worse, I didn't come prepared with any questions.

Man, talk about obnoxious! I know he was put off by me because after he was done with his broadcast, his attitude had shifted. He kept his distance, and while he did throw me in the chair to let me practice for my demo, he didn't offer any feedback. So what was my critical mistake? I realized later that I hadn't gone in there to build a relationship. My heart was in the right place, but I needed to be way more intentional with my behavior by showing humility and respect.

THREE RULES TO MAKING IT COUNT

If you will approach each connection with the idea that you are there to build a relationship, you can avoid that same embarrassment I felt. You can be bold and audacious without being obnoxious. To do this, you just need to follow three simple rules:

1. Listen and Learn
2. Be Humble
3. Add Value

Listen and Learn

Since you're rarely going to impress people with what you tell them about yourself, the rule of "show me—don't tell me" definitely applies when you're making connections. Show people who you are through your actions and attitude rather than listing off your achievements. That means you shouldn't do all the talking. Give people time to teach and share what they know with you. That's the point of you meeting with them in the first place: to learn from them! Go prepared with thoughtful questions to ask, and then be quiet and listen. This will truly speak volumes!

> YOU'RE RARELY GOING TO IMPRESS PEOPLE WITH WHAT YOU TELL THEM ABOUT YOURSELF.

Be Humble

Second, be humble in your posture and tone when you connect with others. Approach them with gratitude for any time and information they're willing to share with you. If you come across as entitled or deserving of their time and attention, not only will you turn them off, but you will miss the chance to build a relationship and miss out on a great opportunity. These folks have the ability to help you get in proximity of your dream job and they deserve your respect and thanks.

Add Value

Ideally when you connect with people, you should add value to them or help them in some way. You could offer to serve or volunteer for their work or organization. Just remember that even the smallest opportunity they give you needs to be met with your best effort and hardest work. You will be surprised by how only a few hours of your time can make a lasting impression on them.

> EVEN THE SMALLEST OPPORTUNITY NEEDS TO BE MET WITH YOUR BEST EFFORT AND HARDEST WORK.

And if you are only meeting them once to connect face-to-face, you can still add value just by valuing them and their time. Everyone enjoys when their opinion or expertise is being sought out. Show how excited you are to get to learn from them. Avoid focusing on your goals and focus on them as a source of knowledge and wisdom. Even small, one-time connections can go a long way in growing you and helping you take the next step forward.

HELPING OTHERS WILL HELP YOU

As you begin building real, genuine relationships with others, remember that this isn't a solo climb. You can't reach the summit alone. It's going to require a whole lot of help from the people around you, so making your connections count is critical! Like I've said already, it will take a lot of patience and intentionality. But the work and time you put into this can lead to some of your greatest opportunities. You have to be humble, and you have to be willing to listen to and learn from others. They have a lot to teach you. Focus first on them and how you can help them before focusing on how they can help you.

In your journey to your dream job, you can have all the passion in the world, but it will still require real audacity and humility to yield the relationships and results you need to get to your goal. Be bold, daring, and fearless as you look for ways to make your connections count. If you can keep in mind that helping others will also help you reach your own summit, you'll find your climb to the top will be more rewarding overall!

CHAPTER 14

SEIZING THE OPPORTUNITY

I will prepare and some day
my chance will come.

—ABRAHAM LINCOLN

The Proximity Principle will bring you face to face with opportunities. That I can promise you. But I can also promise that you're going to need to work really hard to get those opportunities. You first have to put yourself around the right people—professors, professionals, mentors, peers, and producers. Then you've got to find the right places to learn and practice. And when you are finally ready to move on to find a place to perform or grow, you'll have to accomplish one really important thing: landing the interview.

This is where it gets fun. I love helping people who have worked really hard to get to their dream job only to hit a wall when it comes to actually landing an interview. That's exactly where Kristen was the day she called my show. She was frustrated. Kristen told me that she had sent out fifty resumés in five days and still hadn't received a single response. When I pressed her for a little more information, she confessed that she had no personal connection to *any* of the people she'd sent resumés to. She didn't have a single friend, acquaintance, friend of a friend, or even a friend of a coworker employed at any of the places she was targeting in her job search. She was feeling completely discouraged and was beginning to question if she'd ever land an interview.

The good news for Kristen was that the lack of response had nothing to do with her personally. Her resumé was just stuck in a gigantic pile with hundreds of other unread resumés! Kristen's problem is extremely common. Nearly every week on my radio show, people call in to express their exasperation over the lack of response they've received to the gazillion resumés they've sent out. But here's the deal. Blasting out your resumé to

BLASTING OUT YOUR RESUMÉ TO PEOPLE YOU DON'T KNOW IS THE WORST WAY TO LAND AN INTERVIEW.

people you don't know is the worst way to land an interview. This just isn't how resumés are supposed to work.

What works is getting in proximity to the right people and the right places. That's what's going to move your resumé to the top of the pile. You *can* leverage your resumé to get interviews for the jobs you want. But it requires two things: the *right resumé* in the *right hands*.

FORGET EVERYTHING YOU'VE BEEN TAUGHT

To create the right resumé, I need you to forget everything you've been taught or you think you know about writing resumés. Why? Because every resumé template you've ever seen is truly awful. You might be thinking, *Surely not every template, Ken! I think my traditional resumé is pretty sharp.* Nope! Your resumé may not be completely terrible, but the way it's currently written isn't going to get you the results you want. But before I tell you what to do on your resumé, let's talk about three things *not* to do.

1. Don't Add Too Much Information
2. Avoid Using Cookie-Cutter Templates
3. Stop Relying on a Piece of Paper

Don't Add Too Much Information

Believe me, it's time to start from scratch. Most resumé templates ask you to add way too much information. And it's tempting to load it up, because you want to make sure hiring managers and producers know that you can do the job. But adding unnecessary details to your resumé makes it overwhelming. Your resumé isn't your life story, so it shouldn't include a list of everything you've ever done. Don't be like Andy from *The Office*. No one cares that you were president of an a cappella group your senior year (especially if that group's name was "Here Comes Treble")! It's simply too much information.

Avoid Using Cookie-cutter Templates

You've also got to avoid the cookie-cutter templates that everyone else is using. Remember, your resumé is sitting in a pile with hundreds of others, and the hiring manager is looking at multiple variations of the same format. If yours looks like everyone else's, it won't capture the hiring manager's attention. Think about your regular commute that you make day after day. It only takes a few days for you to stop noticing the same buildings, same lights, and same signs. Yet if something changes, like a new Mexican restaurant pops up, it catches your eye right away. Imagine the same thing happening to producers as they look at the same exact format through stacks and stacks of resumés! If yours looks different, it may just get pulled out of the stack.

Stop Relying on a Piece of Paper

Okay, last thing. Here's the most important thing you need to do. Let go of the idea that your resumé is "the thing" that's actually going to get you the interview. It's not. You cannot convince anyone to hire you with a piece of paper, no matter how great it is, because producers hire *people* for jobs—not *paper*. So stop relying solely on a document to get you where you want to be.

PRODUCERS HIRE *PEOPLE* FOR JOBS— NOT *PAPER*.

THE RIGHT RESUMÉ

That said, resumés are still a key tool to help put you in proximity of your dream job, so I've designed a unique resumé template that will stand out and highlight your connections to the company you're applying for. You can easily download my free resumé template at kencoleman.com. I really encourage you to try it. Listen, this stuff works!

Remember my caller Kristen from the start of this chapter? Well, she went back to the drawing board. She reworked her resumé and crafted each one she sent out, leading with her connections in those companies. Rather than mailing out fifty at a time, she did her homework. On a super productive day, she sent out five. Her mindset had shifted from working in mass production to hand-crafting each resumé.

When Kristen called back into the show, she reported that she was getting more responses and interviews from her researched and focused approach than she ever did when she was blasting out the traditional resumé template. Eventually she landed an interview for the role she wanted as a controller at a company that was a great fit for her—all because she put the time and intention into building her resumé the right way.

PREPARE TO WIN

After you've put in the work to design hand-crafted resumés, you can expect to hear back from the companies about the opportunities you're applying for. Landing an interview is an exciting next step, but the truth is interviews can be a little bit intimidating. We've all been in those moments where we feel like nerves could take over any second, especially if it's a job we really, really want! When your dream job is on the line, the desire to say the right things and make a good impression can completely rattle you! But did you know that nerves are the body's response to opportunity? They give you a burst of energy, and you can harness that energy and use it to prepare to win. As the Hall of Fame basketball coach Bob Knight was fond of saying, "The key is not the will to win—everybody has that. It is the will to *prepare* to win that is important." With that in mind, here are three strategies you'll need to implement to win the interview:

1. Prepare to Perform
2. Present the Best You
3. Follow Up

Prepare to Perform

When you're preparing for an interview, you've got to start at square one: preparation and research. In order to identify specific ways that you can help the organization, you should do your research and discovery well in advance. You should focus your research on the company or organization and the person you're interviewing with.

Researching the company will help you get a clear understanding of the organization. This is such a great way to show you're passionate about the work they do and to make a good first impression. Get familiar with the company's website before the interview. Preparing yourself before the interview will give you confidence, and it will empower you to talk intelligently to the hiring managers about their business. Most importantly, getting answers to relevant questions will help you know pretty immediately if the job is a right fit for you.

Next, you'll want to research the person or people who will be interviewing you. Doing this research allows you to ask meaningful questions about their role and have better conversations during the interview. If you discover that the hiring manager went to Duke University, you can drop a "Go Blue Devils" into the conversation and make a connection that is more personal than professional.

> **WHEN YOU'RE PREPARED TO WIN IN THE INTERVIEW, YOU SHOW HIRING MANAGERS THAT YOU'LL BE PREPARED TO WIN IN THE ACTUAL ROLE!**

This can help loosen up an interview that's feeling a little too formal and help the hiring manager see you as a person with interests beyond just the hiring process.

Now listen to me, your level of preparation is an indication of your dedication and desire. When you're prepared to win in the interview, you show hiring managers that you'll be prepared to win in the actual role!

Present the Best You

You've heard people say, "Don't judge a book by its cover." And while in an ideal world people wouldn't judge each other by first impressions, the reality is they do—and they will. That's a harsh truth, but you've got to understand that in the interview process your first impression matters. The first time the hiring manager lays eyes on you is important. So your job is to present the very best version of you. How do you do that? By focusing on two simple things: appearance and attitude.

Appearance

When it comes to appearance, presenting the best you can be as simple as getting a haircut and wearing clothes that are clean and pressed. Your goal is to match the dress code for the company and role. You don't want to show up wearing a formal suit if the company is a jeans and sneakers sort of place!

In today's world where social media is used by nearly everyone, you can't focus just on your *physical* appearance. Take some time to clean up your *digital* appearance as well. You don't want your college spring break party pictures to keep you from landing an interview for your dream job. And this seems obvious, but I'm going to say it anyway: you've got to delete any pictures, posts, or comments that link you to irresponsible, illegal, or elicit behavior.

> IN AN IDEAL WORLD PEOPLE WOULDN'T JUDGE EACH OTHER BY FIRST IMPRESSIONS, BUT THE REALITY IS THEY DO—AND THEY WILL.

Attitude

Bringing the right attitude to the interview is just as important as your appearance. This is where you've got to turn on the charm. If you have a more laid-back personality, you may feel like you are coming across as fake, but try not to overthink it. You just need to show real energy, a big smile, and a grateful attitude.

During the interview, your sole focus should be on the interviewer. This is also true for phone or video interviews. Those might feel less like a real interview, but they are still your one shot to make an impression.

BRINGING THE RIGHT ATTITUDE TO THE INTERVIEW IS JUST AS IMPORTANT AS YOUR APPEARANCE.

A couple final tips are to never eat, drink, or chew gum during an interview, and, most important, to *always* keep your phone on silent and out of sight. You don't want to be tempted to glance at your phone or pause the conversation every time someone texts you. If you're easily distracted in an interview, the hiring manager may assume you won't stay focused on your job either.

By doing all of these things well, you will present the very best you to the company. So do your homework, take the time to prepare, and knock their socks off by giving them a fantastic first impression.

Follow Up

After preparation and performance comes follow-up. This needs to be done the right way and soon after. This is where some people drop the ball—even if they nailed the actual interview itself. The right way to follow up involves touching base with the relevant people in a series of communications that I like to call the "Touchpoint Timeline." It's a straightforward, step-by-step process that you can use for two things: following up after an interview and thinking through whether or not you want to take the job. You can check out samples of the follow-up notes and questions I recommend using in the Touchpoint Timeline on my website at kencoleman.com.

A GOLDEN OPPORTUNITY

The interview process can be nerve-wracking and intimidating at times. We've all felt overwhelmed by the pressure that comes along with interviews, and most of us have experienced our share of good ones and not-so-great ones. But you don't have to approach the interview process with dread. Instead, you can look at it as a golden opportunity to get in front of people who can literally change your future. If you follow the practices we talked about in this chapter—if you prepare, present your best self, and follow up well—you'll put yourself in a position to win the interview and land your dream job.

If you want to win at any opportunity you encounter in life, you'll want to adopt a proximity mind-set. This is the last practice you'll need to implement on your journey to work that matters, and we're going to talk about it in the final chapter. Keep reading! Finish strong.

CHAPTER 15

ADOPTING A PROXIMITY MIND-SET

Ability is what you are capable of doing.
Motivation determines what you do.
Attitude determines how well you do it.

—LOU HOLTZ

The mind-set of my friend Cody powerfully impacts everyone around him. He is super talented, and he immediately began building his influence within Ramsey Solutions from his first day on the job. Cody was a key member of the team that helped me launch *The Ken Coleman Show*—and, believe me, I needed a lot of help! I honestly couldn't have done it without him. Cody now works in a new position unrelated to the show, yet he still takes time from the responsibilities of his new role to send me useful research or to pass on great ideas that help me improve.

I call Cody's approach to his work and the work of others a "proximity mind-set." He's focused on doing his own job well, but he stays alert and receptive to opportunities to help the organization win as a whole. When he sees the chance to help someone else do well, he doesn't hesitate. Cody's killing it in his role, and his attitude and approach make everyone want to work with him.

THE PROXIMITY MIND-SET

So far in the proximity practices section of this book, we discussed how to create a web of connections, how to make those connections count, how to build a resumé that will land you interviews. This final piece—how to adopt a proximity mind-set—is absolutely crucial. But how do you know when you've adopted a way of thinking? That may seem really abstract and difficult to measure. What does success even look like? It's really not that difficult. When you approach your work with a positive attitude, exceptional effort, and a winning disposition, that's when you know you've adopted a proximity mind-set.

Whether you're starting out in your own zip code, a

place to learn, a place to practice, a place to perform, or a place to grow, you must cultivate this way of thinking. To do so you need to do three things:

1. Know Your Role
2. Accept That Role
3. Maximize Your Role

Let's walk through the steps of a proximity mind-set.

Know Your Role

Your passion for what you do can have a lasting impact on the people around you, but in order to make that kind of impact, you must first know your role. I'm not talking about your *job title* here. To me job titles are essentially meaningless. You've got to find out what's expected of you in your *position.* You need clarity on what the organization wants from you and what your supervisor wants from you. One of the unique things about working at Dave Ramsey's company is that each member's role is clearly defined. All team members have a job description with clear, distinct, and measurable responsibilities. We call it a KRA: Key Results Area. Not every company is this transparent, which can make this part of the process tricky. But even

> YOU NEED CLARITY ON WHAT IT MEANS TO WIN IN YOUR ROLE.

for people whose job descriptions are clearly defined, it's still important to investigate this further. Sit down with your employer, immediate supervisor, or boss and walk through your job description bullet by bullet. You want to get pin-point clarity on what it means to be truly successful in the job you have. I like to call this "winning in your role." If there are any expectations outside of what's on that piece of paper, write them down. You want to know the expectations your boss has for you, no matter how small. Then do some research to get some big-picture context. How do your peers or other professionals achieve results in similar roles? How have those in the role before you performed well? How might you possibly add value above and beyond their performance?

My friend Tim is a great example of how to do this. Tim played college football as a linebacker for a university in the Big Ten Conference and had the chance to try out as an undrafted free agent with a professional football team. When he arrived to work that first day, he asked the coaching staff what their expectations for his role would be if he made it onto the roster of that NFL team. He knew he wasn't going to play linebacker right away like he did in college, so he needed to get clarity on his role as a special teams player, covering punts and kickoffs. He talked with his coaches, stayed late after practice, studied film of the people who were winning on special teams, and asked the veteran players for tips about how he could be more effective. Ultimately Tim was able to determine what his coaches expected from him—what winning looked like—and what he needed to do to go above and beyond as a special teams player. You know what all that extra initiative got him? A place on that NFL roster!

If you're struggling to pin down exactly what's expected of you in your work, my friend Michelle's story may help show you how to cut through the fog. When Michelle joined a local publicity firm, she immediately went to work clarifying her job responsibilities. She knew that her primary role was to generate media stories for the firm's clients. Specifically, she was going to handle radio campaigns. Michelle had to learn everything she could about how to organize, pitch, and follow up on pitched stories—as well as make sure her clients were well-prepared for their interviews.

She outlined every single step it took to pitch a story successfully so that she wouldn't drop a single ball. She even went as far as asking her boss how many interviews she needed to schedule each week to help the firm meet its goals. By being proactive in clarifying her responsibilities, she quickly understood what success looked like in her new job. This freed her up to work effectively to help her team, surpassing her boss's expectations. That's definitely a win! You can help your organization in the same way by getting a clear understanding of the expectations for your role. Then you'll know what winning looks like for you— and you'll be able to get wins for the company as well.

Accept Your Role

Once you know the exact expectations for the job you're in, you need to fully accept that role—no matter where you are in your climb up the mountain. Accepting your role is all about attitude. Honestly, this can be a challenge for all of us at some point because it's human nature to want more. It's completely normal to get distracted from the day-to-day goals because you have your eye on the summit and want to keep climbing. I would even argue that it's not only normal but it's healthy to want to grow into more responsibility and advance up the career ladder. Most employers are looking for people who want to push themselves to grow and improve! But there's also a danger in looking past your current role toward the future.

> EVERY STEPPING STONE HAS THE REAL POSSIBILITY OF BECOMING A CORNERSTONE FOR YOUR LONG-TERM CAREER SUCCESS!

Although it can be tempting to rush ahead and move on from the role you're in, you should never take what you believe is a stepping-stone position for granted. Why? Because every stepping stone has the real possibility of becoming a cornerstone for your long-term career success! While it's great to keep your eye on your ultimate goal, you also have to stay focused on winning in the present. Remember, there are goals to reach in your current position too! Don't be so obsessed with the *next* that you don't focus on the *now*. Because doing the *now* with excellence is the stepping stone that will help you win in the *next*. So how do you do this? How do you fully accept your role? You start by having an attitude of gratitude toward the work right in front of you. No matter how little or mundane the task is, you have to do it with excellence.

Linda, a woman who called into my show one day, told me how focusing on the present got her one step closer to her future. The coolest part of Linda's story is that she wasn't calling to celebrate getting her dream job. She was calling to commemorate a significant win she had at work as a result of changing her mind-set. Linda could see a clear path to the position she really wanted, but she also realized that she had been so focused on looking elsewhere for opportunities that she hadn't focused on her current responsibilities to the best of her ability. She confessed that she hadn't done a great job of embracing her role. Linda made the decision that if she was ever going to move up, she had to change her attitude and really embrace the work that she had in front of her.

So she focused on being grateful for her work and attacking everything she was asked to do with enthusiasm. She stopped treating her job as a stepping stone and instead tried to see it as a cornerstone for growth. And guess what happened? Not only did her boss notice this change, but he was so impressed that he came to her two months later and offered her a new job—a position that was one step closer to her dream role. And this new position came with a $10,000 raise, which was really going to help her meet her financial goals! Linda called in to my show to explain what a dramatic difference it can make if you're simply willing to embrace your role and focus on the present instead of worrying solely about the future.

I can relate to Linda's story of losing a little focus in the here and now and having to hit the reset button. When I came to Ramsey, I gave up hosting my own little radio show in Georgia. Now, I knew beyond a shadow of doubt that I was in the best place for growth and learning, but part of me just missed the daily grind of hosting my own show. And when I first arrived, my role was to emcee live events and host a really great leadership podcast called the EntreLeadership Podcast, which, by the way, I still host today. Working on those two responsibilities was what was expected of me and how I could best help the company win.

One evening I came home from work feeling impatient about where I was in my role and longing to do more. It was one of those days I really missed having my own show. I loved the company and people, and I knew there was a ton of opportunity for my future there, but that day I felt like a little part of me had died. I began to talk to my wife about my frustrations, and she helped to completely turn my attitude around. She reminded me to be grateful for the incredible opportunities that were in front of me at work every day and to be patient and accept my role. My wife was right—and getting back to an attitude of gratitude snapped me out of focusing on the next and helped me focus on the now. You need people like this in your life to give you a reality check and help you refocus. Others who have a proximity mind-set can do this. They can help you see that even when you accept and embrace your current role, that doesn't mean that's it, you're done. You can actually go above and beyond by maximizing your role.

Maximize Your Role

You don't have to wait until you've reached your dream job to maximize your role. In fact, you shouldn't. Maximizing your role is the effort you bring to executing your job. And you can do this in *any* job and in *any* role. You'll just need to look above and beyond your basic job responsibilities—to think beyond just what's best for you to what's best for the people around you. This could look like actively pursuing opportunities to help people in other areas of the organization or simply going the extra mile to help a teammate finish a project that's traditionally out of your lane. If you're going to maximize your role, you can't just

> TO MAXIMIZE YOUR ROLE, YOU CAN'T JUST WAIT AROUND FOR A CHANCE TO MAKE A DIFFERENCE.

wait around for a chance to make a difference. There's nothing that illustrates this idea quite like the story of Carolyn Collins, a high school janitor who worked a few miles outside of Atlanta, Georgia.

A few years ago, Collins was busy doing her job well. Early one morning before school, she was about to take out the trash when she heard knocking on the cafeteria door. She opened the door to find two high school students waiting outside—a brother and sister who were homeless at the time, living out of their mother's car. She brought them inside and gave them food and school supplies. Her heart went out to the students when she realized they were hungry and didn't have anything to eat. Suddenly Collins recognized there was a need in her own school that no one was addressing. She knew she couldn't just sit back and say, "This isn't in my job description." No. She had to take action.

On her drive home from work that day, Collins stopped at the store and spent $200 of her own money on snacks, toiletries, socks, underwear, notebooks, and pencils. The next day she went to the principal's office to explain what had happened the day before and how she planned to help. She got the principal's blessing, and that afternoon, she cleaned out an old storage room near the cafeteria and began stocking the shelves with items. Before the school doors opened the next morning, Collins's "giving closet" was up and running.

Since 2014 any of the school's students who need

items such as food, soap, school supplies, book bags, and clothes can quietly mention it to Ms. Collins, as they call her, and she opens the closet for them and gives them what they need. And if a student needs something that isn't in the closet, she does everything in her power to go out and find it. Carolyn Collins is a beautiful example of someone who looked beyond her job description and everyday responsibilities and saw an opportunity to help others in a practical and life-changing way. Now, as a result, she's impacted an entire high school and its surrounding community![55]

What kind of impact could we make in our work if we each maximized our role like Collins? What sort of difference could we make in our work and our organizations? And in our communities? What could you accomplish if part of your to-do list for every day was to go above and beyond what was simply required of you?

Folks, the practice of adopting a proximity mind-set can reap rewards not only for yourself but for others. Not just for your organization, but for your community. This is where knowing your role, accepting your role, and maximizing your role come together to make a truly winning combination.

CONCLUSION

PRESSING ON

※

It's not the destination. It's the journey.

—RALPH WALDO EMERSON

The famous Scottish mountaineer William Hutchinson Murray, who I mentioned in the introduction, didn't stop after he climbed his first mountain. He looked toward the next challenge and the next—and the next. He was a world-renowned mountain climber, then he went on to make a name for himself as a writer. He was always challenging himself. Always pushing his own limits.

I quoted a passage from him in the introduction, and this piece of it is worth repeating again: "I have learned a deep respect for one of Goethe's couplets: Whatever you can do, or dream you can, begin it. Boldness has genius, power, and magic in it![56]

As I read this, I can't help but reflect back on the first steps of my climb and how hesitant I was to begin. There were times I wanted to draw back, to talk myself out of it. *What if I failed? What if I wasn't good enough or smart enough?* But I ignored the voices of fear and pride, and I began putting one foot in front of the other. I committed to the climb. I chose to be bold. The Proximity Principle has been essential to my journey and has put me around the right people and places that opened doors of opportunity.

Over the course of the book, you have learned how the right people, the right places, and the right practices can help you find the opportunities where you are able to use what you do best to do what you love most. Whenever you arrive at your professional summit—whatever that job may be—you will discover that The Proximity Principle is a way of thinking, a way of acting, a way of living. It's the common factor in the lives of every successful person I have met. And here's the thing: if you're the type of person who has what it takes to make it to the summit of your climb, you're also the kind of person who is going to aspire to continued growth. Once you've ascended that first mountain, you'll look out and see there are more mountains to climb and more exciting challenges ahead.

Why is it so important to me that you reach your full potential? Because you matter—and what you do for work matters. Work is where we will spend an estimated 90,000 hours—one third—of our lives, and so it's deeply important to do meaningful work.[57] You have unique talents and abilities to accomplish things in the world only *you* can do. While most workers approach their jobs with a hopeless, resigned attitude of "watching the clock" or "cashing a check," you've chosen to believe your work has purpose and meaning! That makes all the difference.

On your journey to work that matters, there may be mornings you'll wake up discouraged. You'll be tempted to look up at those risky trails on your climb and feel it's just too far to go and you might not make it. You'll hesitate and want to draw back. There will be days when you'll face rejection. And there will be times when fear and pride knock you down. In those moments, know that you are not alone. I've been in your shoes. And so many others have too. But while fear and pride may get you down temporarily, you cannot let them keep you down. You *can* do this. You have what you need to make the climb. So pick yourself up, dust yourself off, and put one foot in front of the other.

You were created to fill a unique role. The world needs you to fill it.

So set your sights on that one thing you know you were created to do. The work that fires you up and makes you feel alive, and use The Proximity Principle to make it happen.

Press on!

NOTES

1. Jim Clifton, "The World's Broken Workplace," Gallup, June 13, 2017, https://news.gallup.com/opinion/chairman/212045/world-broken-workplace.aspx.
2. William Hutchison Murray, *The Scottish Himalayan Expedition*, (J. M. Dent & Co, 1951).
3. Undiscovered Scotland. "W. H. Murray." https://www.undiscoveredscotland.co.uk/usbiography/m/whmurray.html.
4. Peter Economy, "Steve Jobs on the Remarkable Power of Asking for Help," *Inc.*, June 11, 2015, https://www.inc.com/peter-economy/steve-jobs-on-the-remarkable-power-of-asking-for-what-you-want.html.
5. "Wayne Gretzky, Canadian Hockey Player," *Encyclopedia Britannica*, December 3, 2018, https://www.britannica.com/biography/Wayne-Gretzky.
6. Aine Cain, "'Can You Please Look Away While I Deliver the Rest of the Speech?': Will Ferrell Tells New Grads How to Get Past Their Fear of Failure," *Business*

Insider, May 16, 2017, https://www.businessinsider.com/
will-ferrell-on-finding-success-fear-of-failure-2017-5.

7. Gary Graff, "Don Felder Remembers Tom Petty as
a Friend, Student & 'Fearless' Performer," *Billboard*,
October 3, 2017, https://www.billboard.com/articles
/columns/rock/7988695/don-felder-tom-petty-tribute
-friend-student-gainesville-florida.

8. Helena de Bertodano, "Beautiful Creatures: Viola
Davis Interview," *The Telegraph*, February 11, 2013,
https://www.telegraph.co.uk/culture/film/9832218
/Beautiful-Creatures-Viola-Davis-interview.html.

9. Jack Smart, "The Continued Education of Viola
Davis and Denzel Washington," *Backstage*, January
11, 2017, https://www.backstage.com/magazine
/article/continued-education-viola-davis-denzel
-washington-5211/.

10. David Itzkoff, *Robin*, (New York: Henry Holt and
Co., 2018).

11. "Sir Edmund Hillary," *Hillary Institute*, http://www
.hillaryinstitute.com/sir-edmund-full-bio/.

12. Larry Carroll, "Stars Remember Paul Newman: 'He's
What You Aspire to Be,' Leonardo DiCaprio Says,"
MTV News, September 29, 2008, http://www.mtv.
com/news/1595822/stars-remember-paul-newman
-hes-what-you-aspire-to-be-leonardo-dicaprio-says/.

13. Philip Horne, "M Night Shyamalan Interview: A
New Sense of the Spectacular," *The Telegraph*,
August 11, 2010, https://www.telegraph.co.uk/culture

/film/7930719/M-Night-Shyamalan-interview-a-new
-sense-of-the-spectacular.html.

14. Matt Miller, "Paul McCartney Explains How the
Beatles Wouldn't Exist Without Chuck Berry,"
Beatlesarama.com, March 21, 2017, http:
//beatlesarama.com/paul-mccartney-explains-beatles
-wouldnt-exist-without-chuck-berry/.

15. Jackie MacMullan, "Kobe Bryant: Imitating
Greatness," ESPN, June 4, 2010, http://www.espn
.com/nba/playoffs/2010/columns/story?columnist
=macmullan_jackie&page=kobefilmstudy-100604.

16. Henry Blodget, "Here's the Man Who Inspired Steve
Jobs," *Business Insider*, October 9, 2011, https://www
.businessinsider.com/heres-the-man-who-inspired
-steve-jobs-2011-10.

17. Sheila Eugenio, "7 Reasons You Need a Mentor
for Entrepreneurial Success," August 17, 2016,
Entrepreneur, https://www.entrepreneur.com
/article/280134.

18. Jean Rhodes, "Top 25 Mentoring Relationships in
History," The Chronicle of Evidence-Based
Mentoring, September 13, 2015, https://www
.evidencebasedmentoring.org/
top-25-mentoring-relationships-in-history/.

19. "Exclusive: Oprah on Her Last Conversation with
Maya Angelou," *Entertainment Tonight*, May 30, 2014,
https://www.etonline.com/news/146999_exclusive
_oprah_breaks_news_on_maya_angelou_memorial.

20. Clay Clark, "Why Every Great Business Leader Has A Mentor," *Forbes*, June 20, 2017, https://www .forbes.com/sites/forbescoachescouncil/2017/06/20 /why-every-great-business-leader-has-a-mentor/# 76318ba55374.

21. Financial profile of Warren Buffett, CEO of Berkshire Hathaway, *Forbes*, December 7, 2018, https://www .forbes.com/profile/warren-buffett/#230af24e4639.

22. James C. Price, "Great Mentor Relationships Throughout History," Refresh Leadership, January 13, 2015, http://www.refreshleadership.com/index .php/2015/01/great-mentor-relationships-history/.

23. Bill Gates, "Testing Mattresses with Warren Buffet," *Gates Notes*, June 6, 2017, https://www.gatesnotes .com/About-Bill-Gates/Testing-Mattresses-with -Warren-Buffett?WT.mc_id=20170606173828 _BerkshireMtg2017_BG-TW&WT.tsrc=BGTW &linkId=38416190.

24. Chris Weller, "Bill Gates Says His Mentor Was a 6-foot-7 'Giant' of Global Health Also Named Bill," *Business Insider*, October 11, 2017, https://www .businessinsider.com/bill-gates-discusses-mentor -bill-foege-2017-10.

25. Aimee Groth, "You're the Average of the Five People You Spend the Most Time With," *Business Insider*, July 24, 2012, https://www.businessinsider.com/jim- rohn-youre-the-average-of-the-five-people-you-spend- the-most-time-with-2012-7.

26. Emma Jones, "'I Didn't Get into Movies to Please the Critics': Adam Sandler Interview," *Independent*, August 2, 2013, https://www.independent.co.uk/arts-entertainment/films/features/i-didnt-get-into-movies-to-please-the-critics-adam-sandler-interview-8742294.html.

27. Psalm 27:17.

28. David Wharton, "Send in the Clowns: The Comedy Store keeps the laughs coming as it celebrates its 20th birthday with some of the comedians who got their start there," *Los Angeles Times*, April 12, 2018, https://www.latimes.com/entertainment/la-et-send-in-the-clowns-19920920-story.html.

29. Richard Feloni, "How Jimmy Fallon Made It to *The Tonight Show* Through Exceptional Networking," *Business Insider*, November 6, 2014, https://www.businessinsider.com/jimmy-fallon-networking-key-to-success-2014-11.

30. Brittney Morgan, "Career Advice from Katie Couric," *Business News Daily*, June 9, 2014, https://www.businessnewsdaily.com/6558-katie-couric-career-tips.html.

31. "Katie Couric on Love, Career Highs & Our Next Mayor," *Gotham*, November 14, 2013, https://gotham-magazine.com/katie-couric-on-love-career-and-nycs-next-mayor.

32. "Take a Look Back at Disney in the Year 1923," The Official Disney Fan Club, March 6, 2014, https://d23.com/a-walk-with-walt-disney-1923/.

33. Emily Canal, "How These Co-Founder Cousins Made $20 Million Last Year Bringing Maine Lobster to Food Trucks Around the Country," *Inc.*, April 12, 2018, https://www.inc.com/emily-canal/cousins -maine-lobster-food-truck-business.html.

34. Hoda Kotb, "From Video Clerk to Box Office Icon," *Dateline NBC*, April 25, 2004, http://www.nbcnews .com/id/4817308/ns/dateline_nbc-newsmakers/t /video-clerk-box-office-icon/#.XB2gOi2ZN-U.

35. Bailey Mosier, "Arnie: Palmer Born, Raised and Forever in Latrobe," Golf Channel, September 10, 2014, https: //www.golfchannel.com/article/bailey-mosier /arnie-palmer-born-raised-and-forever-latrobe.

36. Ryan Herrington, "Here's Everyone Who Has Earned More than $1 Million on the PGA Tour this Season," *Golfworld*, August 29, 2018, https://www.golfdigest. com/story/heres-everyone-who-has-earned-more-than -dollar-1-million-on-the-pga-tour-this-season-and-the -number-will-amaze-you.

37. Malcolm Gladwell, *Outliers: The Story of Success*, (New York: Little, Brown and Company, 2008).

38. Mike Reiss, "As Tom Brady Improves Movement, 'Broken-Play' Coach Helps," ESPN, September 4, 2018, http://www.espn.com/blog/new-england -patriots/post/_/id/4814711/a-new-twist-tom-brady -and-the-patriots-broken-play-coach.

39. Mark Medina, "Lakers' Kobe Bryant credits Lower Merion's Gregg Downer for molding his game," *Los*

Angeles Daily News, November 30, 2015, https://www
.dailynews.com/2015/11/30/lakers-kobe-bryant
-credits-lower-merions-gregg-downer-for-molding
-his-game/.

40. Rebecca Johnson, "Why Serena Williams Is Best
Friends with Her Fiercest Competitor," *Vogue*,
March 21, 2015, https://www.vogue.com/article
/serena-williams-april-cover-caroline-wozniacki.

41. Henry Blodget, "I Asked Jeff Bezos the Tough
Questions—No Profits, the Book Controversies,
the Phone Flop—And He Showed Why Amazon Is
Such a Huge Success," *Business Insider*, December 13,
2014, https://www.businessinsider.com/amazons
-jeff-bezos-on-profits-failure-succession-big-bets-2014
-12?r=UK&IR=T.

42. "Jeff Bezos: Founder and CEO of Amazon, Inventor
and Perfecter of Modern E-commerce, Popularizer
of E-reading," *Esquire*, September 25, 2008, https:
//www.esquire.com/news-politics/a5038
/jeff-bezos-1008/.

43. Sara Schaefer, "What I've Learned Performing
Comedy at over 50 College Campuses," *Vulture*,
September 10, 2013, https://www.vulture
.com/2018/09/what-ive-learned-performing-comedy
-at-college-campuses.html.

44. Beth Comstock, "My First Job: This Weakling
Worked the Line and Learned How to Bond,"
LinkedIn, October 28, 2018, https://www.linkedin

.com/pulse/20131028225926-19748378-my-first-job
-this-weakling-worked-the-line-and-learned-how-to
-bond/.

45. Adam Bryant, "Beth Comstock of General Electric:
Granting Permission to Innovate," *The New York
Times*, June 17, 2016, https://www.nytimes
.com/2016/06/19/business/granting-permission-
to-try-something-new.html.

46. "How 6 Olympic Athletes Deal with the Pressure,"
Health, June 10, 2016, https://www.health.com
/mind-body/olympians-handle-stress.

47. "Olympian Michael Phelps: How I Conquered
Pressure," NBC News, June 18, 2018. https://www
.nbcnews.com/better/video/olympian-michael-phelps
-how-i-conquered-pressure-1258216515959.

48. Joe Nowlan, "2017 30 Under 35 Profile: J.D.
Henigman," *Ted Magazine*, April 20, 2018, https:
//tedmag.com/2017-30-under-35-profile-j-d-henigman/.

49. Bridget McCrea, "Recruiting and Retention Series:
Carving out a Growth Path," *Ted Magazine*, March
23, 2018, https://tedmag.com/recruiting-and
-retention-series-carving-out-a-growth-path/.

50. "Watch: 'Best Game I Ever Played In'–Michael
Jordan," ESPN 700, April 2, 2015, https:
//espn700sports.com/nba/watch-best-game-i-ever
-played-in-michael-jordan/?apt_credirect=1.

51. Timothy Bella, "'Just Do It': The Surprising
and Morbid Origin Story of Nike's Slogan," *The*

Washington Post, September 4, 2018, https:
//www.washingtonpost.com/news/morning-mix
/wp/2018/09/04/from-lets-do-it-to-just-do-it-how
-nike-adapted-gary-gilmores-last-words-before
-execution/?noredirect=on&utm_term=.05ae3fd62868.

52. Mark S. Granovetter, "The Strength of Weak Ties,"
The American Journal of Sociology, Vol. 78, No. 6
(May 1973), pp. 1360–1380, https://www.cs.cmu
.edu/~jure/pub/papers/granovetter73ties.pdf.

53. "Why Is Spider Silk so Strong?" *Scientific American*,
July 15, 2002, https://www.scientificamerican.com
/article/why-is-spider-silk-so-str/.

54. "Audacious," Merriam-Webster, Accessed on
December 16, 2018, https://www.merriam-webster
.com/dictionary/audacious.

55. Cathy Free, "This School Janitor Has Quietly Been
Giving Homeless Students Clothes, Soap, and More
from Her 'Giving Closet,'" *The Washington Post*,
September 4, 2018, https://www.washingtonpost.com
/news/inspired-life/wp/2018/09/04/this-school
-janitor-has-been-quietly-been-giving-homeless
-students-clothes-soap-and-more-from-her-care
-closet/?noredirect=on&utm_term=.fe2fbb206c48.

56. William Hutchison Murray, *The Scottish Himalayan
Expedition*, (J. M. Dent & Co, 1951).

57. Jessica Pryce-Jones, *Happiness at Work: Maximizing
Your Psychological Capital for Success*, (Hoboken:
Wiley, 2010).

One question changes everything.

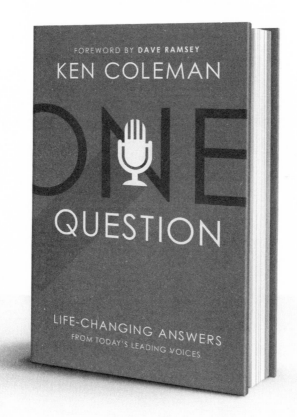

One Question invites you to join Ken Coleman and access today's best and brightest as he delivers carefully crafted questions and collects answers guaranteed to surprise, challenge, and inspire. Learn from Tony Robbins, Jim Collins, Malcolm Gladwell and more.

KENCOLEMAN.COM

DISCOVER WHAT YOU WERE

BORN TO DO.

Check out *The Ken Coleman Show* on your favorite platform to have your career questions answered.